Improving Reading and Study Skills

Ann S. Algier, Keith W. Algier, *Editors*

NEW DIRECTIONS FOR COLLEGE LEARNING ASSISTANCE
KURT V. LAURIDSEN, *Editor-in-Chief*

Number 8, June 1982

Paperback sourcebooks in
The Jossey-Bass Higher Education Series

Jossey-Bass Inc., Publishers
San Francisco • Washington • London

Improving Reading and Study Skills
Number 8, June 1982
    Ann S. Algier, Keith W. Algier, *Editors*

New Directions for College Learning Assistance Series
Kurt V. Lauridsen, *Editor-in-Chief*

New Directions for College Learning Assistance is published quarterly
by Jossey-Bass Inc., Publishers. Subscriptions, single-issue orders,
change of address notices, undelivered copies, and other
correspondence should be sent to *New Directions* Subscriptions,
Jossey-Bass Inc., Publishers, 433 California Street, San Francisco,
California 94104.

Editorial correspondence should be sent to the Editor-in-Chief,
Kurt V. Lauridsen, Director, Student Learning Center,
University of California, Berkeley, California 94720.

Library of Congress Catalogue Card Number LC 81-48565
International Standard Serial Number ISSN 0271-0617
International Standard Book Number ISBN 87589-880-7

Cover art by Willi Baum
Manufactured in the United States of America

Ordering Information

The paperback sourcebooks listed below are published quarterly and can be ordered either by subscription or as single copies.

Subscriptions cost $35.00 per year for institutions, agencies, and libraries. Individuals can subscribe at the special rate of $21.00 per year *if payment is by personal check.* (Note that the full rate of $35.00 applies if payment is by institutional check, even if the subscription is designated for an individual.) Standing orders are accepted.

Single copies are available at $7.95 when payment accompanies order, and *all single-copy orders under $25.00 must include payment.* (California, Washington, D.C., New Jersey, and New York residents please include appropriate sales tax.) For billed orders, cost per copy is $7.95 plus postage and handling. (Prices subject to change without notice.)

To ensure correct and prompt delivery, all orders must give either the *name of an individual* or an *official purchase order number.* Please submit your order as follows:

Subscriptions: specify series and subscription year.
Single Copies: specify sourcebook code and issue number (such as, CLA8).

Mail orders for United States and Possessions, Latin America, Canada, Japan, Australia, and New Zealand to:
Jossey-Bass Inc., Publishers
433 California Street
San Francisco, California 94104

Mail orders for all other parts of the world to:
Jossey-Bass Limited
28 Banner Street
London EC1Y 8QE

New Directions for College Learning Assistance Series
Kurt V. Lauridsen, *Editor-in-Chief*

Contents

Editors' Notes

The rapidly expanding population of students who need academic support continues to confound traditional faculty members. Many have come to recognize that faculty positions are tied to rates of attrition. For that reason, there appears to be at least tacit acceptance of the idea of learning assistance programs. However, instructors seem increasingly willing to help students learn how to learn. The problem of underprepared students in higher education is not going to fade away in the next few years.

This volume of *New Directions for College Learning Assistance* begins with a general philosophy of academic support by Georgine Materniak and an overview of successful programs by Vickie Sanders, Heath Lowry, and William Theimer.

Because this series of sourcebooks is written with practitioners in mind, the remaining chapters deal with methods for enhancing student learning. The authors were asked to interpret their findings in a manner that would make them usable.

John Milton discusses the importance of considering student characteristics in diagnosing study skills problems, especially as these characteristics affect the student's ability to master the art of note-taking.

The growing realization that a lack of reasoning skills can cause reading problems motivates Arthur Whimbey and John Glade to suggest materials and classroom procedures to improve reading comprehension. The authors comment on recent studies of mental activities in intelligence and analytical reasoning, which appear to shed light on the nature and teaching of comprehension processes.

Martha S. Conaway's review of the relationship of attrition and retention of college students prefaces a report of her recent findings on correlations of grade point average, reading, and listening comprehension. She offers a number of practical suggestions for improving students' listening comprehension.

Textbook analysis and the ability to store and retrieve vast amounts of information is the focus of Ann Algier's chapter. The author maintains that instructors should emphasize efficient study strategies that are already available for practitioners. These strategies must be presented in a convincing manner and faithfully implemented by students in a variety of study situations.

Knowing course content and having a clear writing style are not sufficient for performance on essay examinations, according to David Hubin and Susan J. Lesyk. The authors maintain that students need to appreciate examination preparation as a culmination of active learning based on critical analysis, synthesis, and organized thought.

The last two chapters, one by Robert R. Tarvin and Suzanne Teegarden, the other by Ernest W. Tompkins, call attention to the changing population in higher education and make recommendations for the future.

Collectively, the authors of the chapters in this sourcebook represent views from a wide variety of institutions—two- and four-year colleges as well as technical schools.

Ann S. Algier
Keith W. Algier
Editors

Ann S. Algier, associate professor and former chairman of the Department of Learning Skills, Eastern Kentucky University, Richmond, designed and implemented an institutionally supported academic assistance program at EKU in 1969. Vice-president of the Kentucky Council of the International Reading Association, she is the author of Everything You Need to Know About Learning *(Kendall/Hunt, 1979).*

Keith W. Algier is professor of history at Eastern Kentucky University, where he also serves as faculty representative on the institution's Board of Regents. He is a member of the faculty advisory committee to the Kentucky Council on Higher Education and was recently named to the Paper Prize Award Committee for Phi Alpha Theta International History Honorary.

*Study skills are more than techniques; they are a system
for processing, storing, and retrieving information.*

Study Skills: A Practical
Application of
Information-Processing Theory

Georgine Materniak

Psychology is undergoing a revolution. Behavioral theory, which dominated
the field in past decades, is losing its stronghold as cognitive psychology gains
more attention. Psychologists are shifting their focus from the acquisition of
behavior to the processes underlying behavior that explain how the mind
functions. "The field flourishes: The study of human information processing
continues to produce important insights into our understanding of human
mental processes. New phenomena challenge old ideas. New ideas have
advanced our understanding of old phenomena. Each year, new developments enrich our knowledge and widen the scope of behaviors that we can
begin to comprehend" (Lindsay and Norman, 1977, p. v).

The learning assistance field is also changing. During the past decade,
learning specialists functioned primarily as skills practitioners. They concentrated on establishing methods and programs that served student needs and
on introducing traditional institutions of higher education to a holistic
learning philosophy. Although a need for such efforts persists, the continuity
and success of these efforts have changed the learning specialist's self-image.
A new era of professionalism is emerging and with it an interest in identifying
theories that explain the underlying processes of the skills that we teach.

A. S. Algier, K. W. Algier (Eds.). *New Directions for College Learning Assistance:
Improving Reading and Study Skills,* no. 8. San Francisco: Jossey-Bass, June 1982

Unlike the cases of reading, mathematics, and writing, the theoretical foundations of study skills have been little explored. Study skills are multi-disciplinary, and, consequently, they have not been claimed by a particular academic field. In addition, due to their practical emphasis, they have been regarded as unworthy of formal study. However, the revolution in cognitive psychology is changing all this. Psychologists are providing a theoretical base for study skills. By applying this theory, learning specialists can establish professional credibility.

Study Skills: Two Perspectives

The Standard Approach. Traditionally, study skills are taught separately: textbook reading, lecture note-taking, time management, memory and concentration improvement, and test-taking skills. A prescribed method is presented for each skill. Students are told what to do and how to do it. The standard approach produces successful results, but its perspective is limited, and, as a result, the myths abound.

One myth is that study skills are a collection of separate and independent skills. This is simply not true; they are integrated components of a learning system. As with all systems, a problem in one component can be caused by malfunction in another component. For example, poor performance on a multiple-choice test can cause students to assume that they need to learn test-taking skills. Although that may be the case, most students' test problems can be attributed to inappropriate processing of text and lecture information. The standard approach does not emphasize the interactive nature of the study system. Another myth promulgated by the standard approach is that studying is merely activity. By emphasizing the what and how of studying, the standard approach does little to explain why the skills work. The hazards of this approach are that it assumes that students will accept and apply the methods on blind faith, and it also can foster a passive and mechanical approach to learning.

There is no doubt that the standard approach works in spite of its limitations. Until recently, there were no alternatives. We now have a choice.

The Information-Processing Perspective. Study skills are behaviors that reflect underlying cognitive processes. These processes involve taking in, manipulating, storing, and retrieving information. There are different skills because there are different sources: We see, we hear, and we read. But, once we have the information, it is processed by only one system: the brain.

Human information-processing theory is the foundation of all study skills. By incorporating this theory into study skills curriculum, the limitations of the standard approach can be overcome. That is, human information-processing theory provides a rationale as to why study skills work and how they work, a perspective of the interrelationships between components of the study skills system, and a monitor and control for the active processing of information.

Overview of the Human Information-Processing System

Each of us is an information-processing system. We take in data from the environment and process that data as information, which is stored for future use.

Our system consists of three components: a sensory store, short-term memory (STM), and long-term memory (LTM). Information will reach LTM only if it is actively processed through the sensory store and STM. The system, however, is not linear; components interact to assist each other in carrying out their functions.

The Sensory Store. We are continuously receiving data from the environment. In the time that it takes to process the data, the event that produces them will most likely change or terminate. The function of the sensory store is to retain the acquired data long enough to perceive and interpret them. Sensory stores exist for all senses, although research has focused primarily on the visual and auditory stores. The visual store (icon) is estimated to have a duration of one-fourth second, whereas the auditory store (echo) can last for three or four seconds. Sensory data is raw; it is not meaningful information.

Perception is the process of transforming data into information. Pattern recognition processes analyze and interpret sensory data using existing information stored in LTM. In addition to pattern recognition, perception involves attention. Our capacity to attend to all available sensory data is limited by attention. Attention enables us to filter out unnecessary and extraneous data and to select only data that are important. The limitations of attention have been explained by two theories: data limitation and resource limitation. The example of a cocktail party can illustrate these theories. Conversations across the room cannot be attended to because of the poor quality of sound (data limitation). Although conversations immediately surrounding us can be heard clearly, we are unable to attend to each conversation equally (resource limitation).

In this early stage of processing, we can appreciate the need for active involvement. We must decide the importance of what is being perceived so that attention can be allocated. If the data are attended to and perceived within the duration of the sensory store, they will be transferred to STM. Without processing, information is lost.

Short-Term Memory. After surviving the sensory component, information is transferred to STM for further processing. STM, which has a duration of about one-half minute, has two functions: storage and work.

STM has a storage capacity for about seven pieces of information. Information loss—forgetting—can be caused by overloading the capacity (displacement theory) or by exceeding the time duration (decay theory). Rehearsal of information stored in STM prevents forgetting. There are two types of rehearsal: maintenance and elaborative. Maintenance rehearsal—repetition—recycles information back into STM to combat decay. Elaborative rehearsal methods, such as chunking, organizing, and relating information, combines pieces of information into units. Since each unit can occupy one cell of STM, elaborative rehearsal prevents decay and displacement. Elaborative rehearsal utilizes information stored in LTM to perform manipulations on STM information. The manipulation of STM information is controlled and monitored by the working function. Working memory is consciousness. It controls what you are aware of at this moment. During elaborative rehearsal, it is responsible for extracting the information needed from LTM and for manipulating what is stored in STM.

Active processing is the key to STM information survival and its transfer into LTM. Elaborative processes expedite transfer, because they link LTM with STM. Maintenance rehearsal is risky as a transfer process; until there is an attempt to recall, it is difficult to determine if the information has just beeen recycled into STM or if it has been stored in LTM. And, if repetition does "burn" the information into LTM, there may be retrieval problems.

Long-Term Memory. Unlimited amounts of information can be permanently stored in the LTM data base. LTM can be thought of as a vast network of memory traces that are organized and linked together. This network contains related and meaningful pieces of information that form concepts (semantic memory). Tied into the network are memories of specific events or experiences (episodic memory) and images (visual memory).

How the information is stored affects the retrieval accuracy and efficiency. When new information is brought into LTM, elaborative rehearsal methods incorporate the information into the existing data base and increase the strength of the memory trace. The information can be located and accessed for retrieval. Maintenance rehearsal can "burn" the information into LTM, but it does not strongly link or organize the information into the data base. Locating the information at some later time may be difficult if not impossible.

The concept of forgetting in LTM is different from that of forgetting in STM. In STM, forgetting is caused by information loss. In LTM, the information exists, but it cannot be located. There are two theories of LTM forgetting. Retrieval failure, one theory of LTM forgetting, is caused by inappropriate storage methods. If information is not consciously placed in the data base, there is no organized strategy for searching and locating the information, and retrieval failure is the result. The second theory of LTM forgetting, the interference theory, is concerned with competition between traces. When the mind is attempting to retrieve certain information, the trace of another memory can become active and inhibit the retrieval of the desired information. Interference theory holds that forgetting is caused by the dominance of a strong trace over a weaker trace. There are two types of interference: proactive and retroactive. Proactive interference occurs when an older trace inhibits the memory of a newer trace. Retroactive interference occurs when a newer trace inhibits the retrieval of an older trace.

In spite of the fact that retrieval sometimes fails, the amount of information that can be retrieved and the way in which retrieval is accomplished are quite remarkable. Because information contained in the data base is cross-catalogued in different forms (semantic, episodic, and visual), retrieval can involve all the various parts of the data base. For example, an image can serve as a cue for retrieving a memory of a particular experience (episode), which in turn can trigger the memory of meaningful (semantic) information gained from the experience. Thus, it is not surprising that retrieval is also an active process.

Applying Information-Processing Theory: Some Examples

Information-processing theory can be used to interpret the underlying processes of all study skills. I will limit my discussion and illustrations to the most predominant study problems that I have observed in my work with students at the University of Pittsburgh.

Many students, from undergraduates to professional graduate school students, judge the quality of studying on two criteria: the amount of time invested and the number of repetitions performed. Their past educational experiences have taught them the old adage, "If at first you don't succeed, try, try again." Told by their teachers that they should study harder, students simply put in more time. However, an understanding of information-processing theory can help students to de-emphasize the value of time and repetition and to evaluate their learning by the quality of the information processes that they employ. Here are a few examples of the insights that contribute to this change.

Distributed Practice. A fundamental principle of organizing study time is that distributed practice is better than mass practice. This principle can be applied to time (three one-hour periods are better than one three-hour period) or to the amount of material (break up a thirty-page chapter into smaller units). The advice is sound. Why does it work?

One explanation of why distributed practice works is based on the combined effects of proactive and retroactive interference. In the first part of a study session, the mind is alert, and memory traces that are formed are strong. However, the traces of material learned in the middle portion of the period are weaker and inhibited by the earlier traces. The traces of material learned at the end of the session are fresh and retroactively can inhibit the information studied just prior to the end of the session. The result is that memory is strong for the material studied at the beginning and end of the session. Most of the forgetting that occurs involves the material studied in the middle portion.

Learning in small segments decreases the amount of material and therefore equalizes the formation of memory traces. The dual effect of proactive and retroactive interference is decreased. Most students can relate this notion to their experiences. They acknowledge that they tend to forget the middle portions of a chapter, a lecture, or a study session. Understanding why this common experience occurs provides a convincing argument for distributed practice. In addition, students can relate the concept to methods for managing time and study material.

Mnemonics. Mnemonics are memory devices used to learn things that have no inherent meaning—for example, the order of the planets. Sometimes referred to as tricks, they are in fact valid elaborative rehearsal techniques.

Teaching students how to use the method of loci or key-peg system of mnemonics can be a very enjoyable activity. More importantly, students can use the mnemonic experience to identify and analyze the underlying processes and principals of elaborative rehearsal.

Organizing Information from Text and Lectures. Students can be introduced to a variety of note-taking styles, including the Cornell (Pauk, 1974), Statement pie (Hanau, 1974), organic study (Buzan, 1974), and terrain map (Fenker and Mullins, 1981) systems, to provide them with options for organizing different kinds of subject matter and for accommodating different learning styles. Although each system has a unique style, students should be aware that all these systems incorporate the fundamental processes of elaborative rehearsal. Information is cognitively organized, classified, associated, and related. Notes are visual representations of the LTM network and serve as a record for reviewing and strengthening memory traces.

It is interesting to note that the concept of networks is being incorporated into note-taking systems. The note-taking forms suggested by Buzan (1974) and Fenker and Mullins (1981) are essentially cognitive maps that reflect a semantic network. Once they have an awareness of the theoretical notions from which these systems are derived, students are more likely to implement these forms of note-taking as part of their study process.

Summary

Incorporating information-processing theory into the standard study skills curriculum enables students to understand why the suggested study procedures work, to identify the causes of study problems, and to formulate appropriate solutions. Students perceive studying as a process that produces predictable results, not as a time-consuming activity that may or may not work in achieving the goal of learning. Further, "these new conceptions characterize learners as active information processors, interpreters, and synthesizers. Students who know how to use effective strategies to organize and monitor learning, memory, and information retrieval can take greater responsibility for their own learning and become more instrumental in adapting the learning environment to fit their individuals needs and goals" (Weinstein, 1982, p. 6).

The implications are equally important for the learning assistance profession. The vitality of learning assistance can be attributed to the combined efforts of specialists from many disciplines. Our field is rich because we have integrated diverse perspectives into a common philosophy. However, if the field is to evolve into a profession, it must have a theoretical base that can be shared by all learning specialists. The theory of human information processing may be the answer. It encompasses problem solving and decision making, perceptual and neural processes, and language, all of which are directly related to the work of mathematics, learning disabilities, and reading specialists.

If we can share a common philosophy and theory, our profession will become unified and strong. If we couple our practical experiences with theoretical knowledge, learning assistance professionals can make a great contribution to the pursuit of understanding human cognition.

References

Buzan, T. *Use Both Sides of Your Brain.* New York: Dutton, 1974.
Fenker, R. M., and Mullins, R. *Stop Studying and Start Learning.* Fort Worth, Texas: Tangram Press, 1981.
Hanau, L. *The Study Game: How to Play and Win.* New York: Barnes & Noble, 1974.
Lindsay, P. H., and Norman, D. A. *Human Information Processing: An Introduction to Psychology.* New York: Academic Press, 1977.
Pauk, W. *How to Study in College.* Boston: Houghton Mifflin, 1974.
Weinstein, C. "Learning Strategies: The Metacurriculum." *Journal of Developmental and Remedial Education,* 1982, 5 (2), 6–10.

Georgine Materniak, assistant coordinator of the University of Pittsburgh Learning Skills Center, is responsible for study skills instruction and paraprofessional training. She is past chairperson of the American College Personnel Association Commission XVI, Learning Centers in Higher Education, and founder of the Association of Learning Centers in Higher Education of Western Pennsylvania.

The characteristics of successful college reading-study programs
are examined to determine what constitutes an effective program.

A Look at Successful College Reading Programs

Vickie Sanders
Heath Lowry
William Theimer

How to integrate findings and research data about reading and make practical use of them was the problem addressed by researcher Gene Glass when he proposed the techniques of meta-analysis to synthesize research results (Glass, 1976; Glass and Smith, 1977). In his presidential address to the American Educational Research Association, Glass (1976) contended that reading research had been systematically reviewed, abstracted, and surveyed for years but that the all-important integration of findings was rare. Because he saw a need for such integration, Glass proposed a method for synthesizing analyses, which he called *meta-analysis,* after the Greek word *meta,* meaning *above* or *beyond.* Currently, the term is used to refer to statistical analysis of results from a large number of individual studies for the purpose of comparing and integrating their findings. Meta-analysis allows practitioners to have a much better perception of an effect over many different situations and under many different conditions, because it combines the effects obtained by many studies of a particular effect and compares them to control situations. Typically, findings are based on data collected from large numbers of participants in studies conducted in various parts of the country, which gives greater confidence in results of the eventual sythesis than one

A. S. Algier, K. W. Algier (Eds.) *New Directions for College Learning Assistance:*
Improving Reading and Study Skills, no. 8. San Francisco: Jossey-Bass, June 1982

usually obtains from one research study with between thirty and one hundred participants.

The first such integration of college reading-study literature was performed by Sanders (1979, 1981). In a dissertation (Sanders, 1979) and an article (Sanders, 1981), she presented the statistical results of an extensive analysis of research reports and dissertations published between 1960 and 1977 relating to the effectiveness of college reading and study programs. Statistically significant composite gains in reading rate, in comprehension, and in grade point averages were found for the 6,140 students who participated in college reading-study programs or who served as controls. The average student who took part in a college reading program was found to be better off than 83 percent of nonparticipating students. Unexpected but significant benefits in grade point average (GPA) gains were found, with participating students achieving a .37 GPA advantage over nonparticipants. Subsequent long-term GPA advantage was not examined by Sanders. Thus, college reading-study instruction did make a difference in students' reading rate, comprehension, GPA, and it was evident in other cumulative benefits.

It is comforting to know that college reading-study instructors can cite research to indicate that our services provide opportunity for measurable academic benefits to the students who attend our classes. However, it behooves us to ask what else the meta-analysis tells us about the content of our courses and about the elusive operational factors, like the optimum number of classes per semester, the length of time in class, and the duration of the program? What operational and content factors maximize the measurable changes produced by such programs? As administrators and faculty examine cost-effectiveness and budget accordingly, what is taught and how it is presented becomes even more crucial to program developers and program directors. In this chapter, additional information from Sanders's meta-analysis will be used to show the differences in course content and operational methods among programs included in the meta-analysis.

Procedure of the Meta-Analysis

In the original study (Sanders, 1979), an extensive computer search of college reading-study skills literature was conducted, and a list of 676 bibliographic entries published between 1960 and 1977 were identified and examined. From these entries, sixty-six studies that reported data in quantifiable terms and that appeared to meet the minimum research criteria established for the study were selected. However, only twenty-eight of these studies actually used adequate controls and maintained satisfactory validity or provided the necessary outcome statistics. These twenty-eight studies reported mean gains between treatment and comparison groups on one or more of five variables: changes in reading rate, comprehension, grade point average, vocabulary, and study habits. These studies involved 6,140 students who were either enrolled in reading-study programs or who served as controls during the years examined. These twenty-eight studies were the basis of the meta-analysis. This number was considerably smaller than that anticipated by the researcher, and it was smaller than the model set by Glass. Subsequently, however, Glass and Smith (1979) have stated that the number of studies required for a meta-analysis does not have to be large. He and Smith (Glass and Smith, 1977) confounded the results of their study on counseling by mixing subjective data with objective data. Sanders's studies have maintained the strict selection procedures originally stated by Glass as necessary if good information are to be obtained. In the area of reading in particular, it is important to follow his dictum: "In educational research, we need more scholarly effort concentrated on the problem of finding the knowledge that lies untapped in completed research studies. This endeavor deserves higher priority now rather than adding a new experiment or survey to the pile" (Glass, 1976, p. 4). Sanders's study was an endeavor to find the untapped knowledge that lay in the studies reviewed. As in much other educational research, the results have not been well reported, and much needed information has been omitted—information that enables us to know the variables that appear to be most salient in improving reading and studying skills. Although the studies that were reviewed were not as complete as we would have liked, they did contain information about relevant variables. This chapter summarizes the information about variables described, but it was not possible to treat them statistically, because of the small number reporting in each of the categories.

The meta-analysis technique was used to test for effect size (ES), and the variables identified were those that produced the greater benefit; thus, they are related to program content. Unfortunately, because no studies to date have examined each of these variables separately, we can only recommend that these variables should be included in good reading-study programs. It is hoped that identification of these variables as important in producing positive changes in reading will lead others to conduct studies in which they are tested and controlled. When research is reported in terms of program content variables that relate to beneficial effects, then we will be able to identify good reading-study programs by their content. Of course, we must hope that this research will be reported in detail.

It is also likely that many excellent programs in colleges and universities have not reported experimental data in quantifiable terms. As a result, their programs were not considered or included in this study. A case in point was the reading-study program at Harvard, perhaps one of the oldest in this country, which was described by Hodgins (1970), but Hodgins's description did not report experimental data.

Research Limitations

Interesting questions arise about research quality and the conditions that limit the pursuit of doctoral degrees. It is not our intent to discuss research quality in this article; however, serious deficiencies in reporting what actually transpired in the college reading courses were encountered. Reporting deficiencies were anticipated in the published literature, largely as a result of space limitations. Surprisingly, they were also encountered in "complete," unpublished dissertations. In some cases, adequate descriptions of the student population were omitted, as well as descriptions of course content, method of student selection, frequency of class meetings, and number of class sessions. A few investigators gave no indication at all of program content or dismissed course descriptions with broad catalogue-type generalizations identifying the course as one in "college reading skills" or "skills designed to benefit college students." While such descriptions can be appropriate in catalogues, and while one can assume that any reading-study course would include beneficial reading-study skills, such ambiguity in reports of professional endeavors was unfortunate. More precision in this area would enable practitioners, program developers, and investigators to know the content of a given course, what made it different from others and what treatments contributed to the program outcomes reported.

Herman (1972) perhaps reflected the thinking of many when he concluded: "A general description of a college reading improvement program is impossible, primarily because too many differences exist among programs. There is little agreement on the type of student enrollment, length of the program, methods and materials used for instruction, and program evaluation. The only aspect common to all programs is the basic goal of helping the student become better able to handle his academic work" (Herman, 1972, p. 2). However, he then proceeded to provide one of the most complete accounts of a college reading program that the author encountered during her research. Herman included an almost verbatim record of class instruction and student lessons utilized. Other researchers support his position that, because college reading-study instruction exhibits such diverse and complex patterns of organization and measures of success, research can only identify trends (Devirian, Enright, and Smith, 1975; Harshbarger and Harshbarger, 1976; Huslin, 1975).

In contrast to this viewpoint, Fairbanks (1974, 1975) addressed the question of diversity by examining the content and operational aspects of successful programs. As a result, she was able to identify twenty-eight content factors and seventeen operational factors in sixty-six well-designed research studies that she investigated. The twenty-eight content factors were consolidated into six categories for the research being reported here, while the seventeen operational factors were reduced to fifteen. These factors were the independent variables utilized in the research. Fairbanks's listing should provide subsequent investigators with guidance and direction for the descriptive aspects of program reporting (Figures 1 and 2).

The majority of studies did not report either content or operational factors well enough to allow conclusive findings to be drawn. Several signifi-

Figure 1. Fairbanks and Sanders Content Factors Compared

Fairbanks *Content Factors*	*Sanders* *Modified Content Factors*
1. Main idea	1. *Word study, vocabulary*
2. Analyzing paragraphs	Affixes, roots
3. Setting up purposes	Etymology
4. Recognizing inferences	Dictionary study
5. Drawing conclusions	Note cards, word lists
6. Differentiating fact and opinion	Synonyms
7. Reading charts and graphs	Word attack
8. Outlining	
9. Sequencing ideas	2. *Study skills*
10. Summarizing, notetaking	Listening
11. Context clues	Using the library
12. Affixes, roots	Scheduling time
13. Etymology	Examination preparation
14. Dictionary study	Reading charts and graphs
15. Note cards, word lists	
16. Synonyms, antonyms	3. *Note-taking*
17. Word attack	Outlining
18. Reading in literature	Sequencing ideas
19. Reading in mathematics	Summarizing, note-taking
20. Reading in sciences	Content clues
21. Reading in social sciences	
22. Flexibility in rate	4. *Critical reading skills*
23. Acceleration	Main idea
24. Mechanics in rate	Analyzing paragraphs
25. Listening	Setting up purposes
26. Using the library	Recognizing inferences
27. Scheduling time	Drawing conclusions
28. Examination preparation	Differentiating fact and opinion
	5. *Reading in content areas*
	Reading in literature
	Reading in mathematics
	Reading in sciences
	Reading in social sciences
	6. *Rate and flexibility*
	Flexibility in rate
	Acceleration
	Mechanics in rate

cant correlations were obtained from portions of studies where reporting was more complete. These correlations indicated slightly greater effectiveness for programs reporting inclusion of the six program content factors (PCF) listed earlier and for programs that included diagnostic and participatory instructional methods. The deficiency of program reporting was a serious limitation in meta-analysis. More precise reporting of both content and

16

Figure 2. Fairbanks Program Operational Factors as Used in Sanders Study

1. Tests used diagnostically
2. Students informed of strengths and weaknesses
3. Student participation in planning
4. Student participation in evaluation
5. Use of time for lecture and demonstration
6. Use of time for discussion
7. Use of time for practice: group needs
8. Use of time for practice: individual needs
9. Group size
10. Number of class meetings
11. Length of meetings: hours
12. Duration of program: number of weeks
13. College credit given
14a. Program compulsory
14b. Program voluntary
15. Total hours of instruction

operational procedures would facilitate further evaluation and analysis. Any model reading-study program must remain conjectural until research provides more complete data.

Awaiting that happy day, we can say here that analysis of programs which report greater gains provides some guiding principles for practitioners and program developers. The following recommendations are neither totally supported nor contradicted by the research. They are based upon the professional judgment of the investigator (Sanders, 1979) at the conclusion of the study, which includes a complete listing of programs that provided both adequate reporting and significant gains. In the following paragraphs, characteristics of successful programs are described. Programs are grouped by student population, since each student population appears to have distinct characteristics and needs.

Remedial/Corrective Programs

In this category, the population was most frequently described as high-risk, open-admission students, usually freshmen with minimal admitting qualifications who were required or encouraged to participate in the reading-study program. Socioeconomic and educationally disadvantaged students were included. Several groups were selected on the basis of an arbitrarily determined cutoff point; for example, the lower one third of all entering freshmen.

Recommendations. Instruction in word study, study skills, note-taking, critical reading, and content reading should be included, after diagnosis of individual students' difficulties in reading rate, comprehension, and word attack skills. Limited attention to increasing students' reading rate may be justified under certain circumstances, but it should not be a major emphasis of the program.

Required program attendance and use of diagnostic-prescriptive application techniques appears to enhance efficiency in remedial/corrective programs. Adjunct counseling services as part of the diagnostic process can prove beneficial. The context should stress the relationships of study skills, motivation, and counseling.

Programs should continue for several months, preferably for one semester. One-hour class periods should be scheduled two or three times weekly. Some form of credit recognition should be granted. While discussion methods appear to prove beneficial, considerable emphasis should be given to practical methods for transferring newly acquired reading-study skills to other content areas where students experience academic challenges. Critical reading practice with actual college course materials should be included in both small-group and individual sessions.

Academic Support Programs

In this group, second-semester freshmen and sophomore students on some form of academic probation were the usual target population examined. A broad range of predicted potential student achievement scores was noted as grounds for selection by several investigators. Usually, below-acceptable grade performance or low motivation was the common identifying criterion used to select students. Academic support programs included both volunteer and required-attendance participants

Recommendations. Programs should provide opportunity for diagnosis, self-assessment, or both prior to prescriptive instruction, which should be designed to remediate deficiencies that can have contributed to the academic difficulty. Some opportunity for supportive counseling services appears to be beneficial.

Limited course loads, combined with both academic skills instruction and supportive counseling intervention, appear to be beneficial to students on academic probation. Required participation does not appear to limit program effectiveness in this category, but it should be investigated further.

Developmental Programs

This category included programs designed for or open to all entering freshmen or other interested college students. Some students were advised to improve their reading or study skills; others wanted to do so. A few programs excluded top quantile-achieving students, using entry college admission test scores as the criteria for exclusion.

Recommendations. Developmental programs should be voluntary, rather than required. Instruction should be provided in critical reading study skills, content reading, and rate, with some attention to word study in an overall developmental approach designed for all interested students, not limited to entering freshmen. Diagnosis and remediation for students with deficient rate and comprehension problems appear to produce the greatest benefits. Research has shown that students with slow reading rate spend disproportionate amounts of time reading (Grob, 1970).

Diagnostic-participatory instructional methods appear to be most effective. This supports Fairbanks's recommendation regarding involvement of student participants in all phases of the program. Developmental programs meeting two to three times weekly for less than one semester appeared to be more effective. Individual and group practice with actual college reading materials should be provided, and students should be able to receive professional assistance or guidance as needed.

Three of the six guidelines identified by Fairbanks (1973) were supported by this investigation: First, college students participating in a college reading improvement program should be made aware of their specific difficulties in reading and the means by which they can correct them. Second, involvement of the college students participating should be encouraged in all phases of the program: diagnosis, evaluation, and skills practice oriented to their particular needs. College reading-improvement programs should be geared to meet the needs of individuals, through options, individualized assignments, or both. Care should be taken to avoid depersonalization of the program.

Conclusion

College reading-study programs continue to proliferate on campuses across the nation. Different population groups are served, and programs logically must differ. The nature of this difference is not yet clear from a review of the available research. Many people seem to think that the difference is so obvious that it does not need to be explained. Yet, no systematic and general improvement in reading-study skills instruction can occur until the variables that increase these skills have been identified.

Goethe is reported to have said at age seventy: "I have spent my lifetime learning to read." Perhaps reading professionals are now ready to accept this position: Reading skills acquisition is a lifetime proposition, as appropriate in college as in elementary school. We do not need to apologize for our subject, but we do have to articulate what a truly effective program really includes.

References

Devirian, M. C., Enright, G., and Smith, G. "A Survey of Learning Progam Centers in U.S. Institutions of Higher Education." In R. Sugimoto (Ed.), *College Learning Skills*

Today and Tomorrowland: Proceedings of the Eighth Annual Conference of the Western College Reading Association. Los Angeles: Western College Reading Association, 1975 (ED 117 680).

Fairbanks, M., and Snozek, D. "Checklist of Current Practices in Reading and Study Skills Programs for College Students." Paper presented at the 17th annual meeting of the College Reading Association, Silver Spring, Md., November 1973 (ED 088 020).

Fairbanks, M. "The Effect of College Reading Improvement Programs on Academic Achievement." In P. L. Nacke (Ed.), *Interaction: Research and Practice for College-Adult Reading; Twenty-Third Yearbook of the National Reading Conference.* Clemson, S.C.: National Reading Conference, 1974.

Fairbanks, M. "Relationship Between Research Control and Reported Results of College Reading Improvement Programs." In G. H. McNinch and W. D. Miller (Eds.), *Reading: Convention and Inquiry; Twenty-Fourth Yearbook of the National Reading Conference.* Clemson, S.C.: National Reading Conference, 1975 (ED 116 148).

Grob, J. A. "Reading Rate and Study-Time Demands on Secondary Students." *Journal of Reading,* 1970, *13* (4), 285–288.

Glass, G. "Primary, Secondary and Meta-Analysis of Research," *Educational Researcher,* 1976, *5* (10), 3–8.

Glass, G., and Smith, M. L. "Meta-Analysis of Psychotherapy Outcomes Studies." *American Psychologist,* 1977, *32* (9), 752–760.

Glass, G. V., and Smith, M. L. *Meta-Analysis of Research on the Relationship of Class Size and Achievement.* San Francisco: Far West Laboratory for Educational Research and Development, 1979 (ED 168 129).

Harshbarger, M., and Harshbarger, L. *A Survey of Current Practices in College Reading Improvement Courses Offered by Four-Year, Degree-Granting Public Institutions in the Midwest.* Muncie, Ind.: Ball State University, 1976 (ED 123 601).

Herman, J. "The Effect of a Reading Improvement Program upon Academic Achievement in College." Unpublished doctoral dissertation, University of Connecticut, 1972.

Hodgins, R. "The Text is the Adversary." *Teacher's College Record,* 1970, *72* (1), 7–22.

Huslin, R. A. "What's Happening in College and University Developmental Reading Programs: Report of a Recent Survey," *Reading World,* March 1975, 202–214.

Sanders, V. H. "A Meta-Analysis: The Relationship of Program Content and Operation Factors to Measured Effectiveness of College Reading-Study Programs," Unpublished doctoral dissertation, University of the Pacific, 1979.

Sanders, V. H. "College Reading Studies: Do They Make Any Difference?" *Proceedings of the Thirteenth Annual Conference,* Western College Reading Association, 1981.

Vickie Sanders, Ed. D., is adjunct professor, School of Education, and former director of the Academic Skills Center, University of the Pacific. She is an active consultant for adult reading programs and is currently teacher-reading specialist, Stockton Unified Schools.

Heath Lowry, Ed. D., is professor of education and director of the Reading Clinic, University of the Pacific. He directed the study of which this is a partial report. He is immediate past president of the California Reading Association and active in presenting contemporary reading issues.

William Theimer, Ph.D., is professor of educational and counseling psychology, University of the Pacific. He is past president of the California Educational Research Association, and he is active in evaluation of reading programs and individual student assessment procedures.

By thoroughly searching out characteristics of students' attitudes and backgrounds, course demands, materials, and study strategies, we can show students how to learn for themselves.

What the Student and the Educator Should Have Done Before the Grade: A Questioning Look at Note-Taking

John Whitney Milton

Magic—that is what many students want: interesting classes that entertain as well as edify; an easy, foolproof way to do the hard job of studying; high grades; honor degrees. In response, educators smile or sigh. Studying, as everyone knows, is labor. And labor can be painful. So educators lay out the recommendations: "Underline in your textbooks. Take notes over them. Take notes over lectures, too. Write outlines. Do extra reading. Read with good lighting. Plan each day (and week, and semester). Study more. Work harder." Tutors, counselors, and other helpers explain and urge, scold and plead: "See this topic sentence. Survey before you read. Participate in class. The point of the assignment is this. Watch me work the problem. Take notes. Study more. Work harder."

We tend to seek an easy, foolproof way to do the hard job of teaching. Instruction can be stripped down to lists and acronyms, which take on a life of their own, independent of the concepts and behaviors they are supposed to represent. "SQ3-R" becomes not a complex method of reading—one to be taught over weeks and months—but sacred symbols to be intoned over

A. S. Algier, K. W. Algier (Eds.). *New Directions for College Learning Assistance: Improving Reading and Study Skills,* no. 8. San Francisco: Jossey-Bass, June 1982

students' heads as if to confer a blessing. "Read this handout. Practice what it says. See you next week as a born-again reader."

So, what can educators do? They can consult the experts, of course. Researchers come on the scene, run some studies, and publish the results. What can they tell us about note-taking? A number of articles on this study skill have appeared in recent years. However, the experts are not unanimous on anything about note-taking—including, most fundamentally, whether it works, whether it enhances learning. The answers are mixed.

Fundamental Questions About Note-Taking

To make sense of this situation, let us consider some specific issues connected with note-taking. This will dispel the illusion that note-taking is a simple activity that one can take sides for or against. A convenient starting point is provided by Carrier and Titus (1979), who reviewed studies of a decade. They used the available research to attempt to answer eight questions: Is the act of taking notes useful? What are the criteria for good notes? Are externally provided notes as effective as self-generated notes? When should notes be taken? What are the effects of allowing learners to review notes before an exam? What is the relationship between test mode and test interval expectancies, note-taking strategies, and performance? How does organizational structure of the material to be learned influence note-taking? What individual differences are important in note-taking?

The best answer to all these questions appears to be: It depends. Carrier and Titus could muster no ringing statement of firm conclusions. The available evidence, they said, was enough to "suggest" that "while the process of taking notes is useful, being able to review notes later is more crucial to performance on a variety of learning tasks" (Carrier and Titus, 1979, pp. 310–311). This carefully qualified statement is followed by recommendations for future research on note-taking. This research should take into account, they said, the quality of student notes, not just the quantity; it should base studies on longer presentations of material, not on the short ones used most often so far; it should select material typical of school lessons, not the high-interest material usually employed in such studies; it should include the variety of vehicles of information now available to students, such as television, film, programmed instruction, and computers, not just lectures and written text; and it should investigate how students actually use notes in ordinary studying, not merely in the specialized research situation.

It is both accurate and fair to Carrier and Titus to say that other reviewers of the same research might well have asked different questions and reached different conclusions. For our purposes, it suffices to show that there is no magic, not even in research. How do we respond to this uncertainty? Fortunately, a number of insights have emerged from the research on study skills conducted by psychologists and educators, and these insights show promise of enabling educators to assist students in using their own resources to the best advantage. First, we will discuss certain concepts. Then, we will consider what they tell us about note-taking.

Metacognition

The first concept, metacognition, has been discussed by Flavell (1978) as knowledge that focuses on any cognitive activity or that controls cognition while it is going on. This concept relates two different ideas: knowledge and regulation. The first idea, knowledge of cognition, includes thinking about thinking as an abstract activity. It enables one to examine oneself as a thinker. This idea relates to the purpose of education in affirming that students recognize (or that they can learn to recognize) that cognitive processes are required to meet academic demands. For example, students usually know which aspects of their studying are hard or easy, and they can often state why: The specialized terminology is unfamiliar, the organization of material is confusing, the main points are difficult to isolate, the reasoning presented in the lecture or textbook assumes background that they do not have.

The second idea, regulation of cognition, then comes into play. When students run into trouble, they are in a position to do something to get themselves out of the trouble. Proficient students do just that. They even think ahead to predict where they will encounter difficulties and take steps to minimize them.

The concept of metacognition has been attacked as imprecise, faddish, and unnecessary (Marshall and Morton, 1978). It is true that educators early in the century recorded descriptions of studying that today would be considered metacognitive. However, the theoretical controversy can be left to the specialists, while practitioners working directly with students can use the concept to enhance learning with confidence.

Metacognition in Everyday Life. Note that many processes of metacognition are automatic. Students can often read, write, solve problems, and work in a laboratory. It is when they suddenly run into confusion that they need the advantages of metacognition. Consider the parallel between studying and driving. Everything is fine for experienced drivers as long as they are in familiar territory, the car operates smoothly, they encounter no threat from other drivers, weather, road conditions, or traffic, and they labor under no special constraints of time, stress, or cargo. But, let even one factor become problematic, and drivers shift more attention to the process of driving. Metacognitive processes come into play to assure that the necessary tasks are accomplished. Without these processes, the driver might encounter serious trouble. A similar parallel could be drawn with sports, health, employment, and care of house plants, pets, and babies. As long as people are doing familiar tasks with which they are basically comfortable, they can cope easily with the occasional difficulties.

We may conclude from this that our students are experienced at meta-cognition in many areas of their lives. Although many of them could not articulate the fact, they have used self-monitoring skills to perform well enough in school to reach their present level. Our job is to help students to increase their awareness of self-monitoring, identify the strategies that lead to learning well, and give directed practice that helps students to use the strategies fluently.

Learning Strategies

An extensive literature describes programs designed to teach special strategies for promoting recall of information. According to Brown, Campione, and Day (1981), these programs can be divided into three types: blind training (by far the most common type), in which students are taught a strategy by imitation, without being told explicitly why they are learning it; informed training, in which students are not only taught the strategy but also are told why they are learning, and self-control training, in which students are taught a strategy, its significance is explained, and then students are in-structed in how to employ, monitor, and evaluate that strategy. With blind training, few students use the strategy later. With informed training, the chances are better that students will use the strategy on their own and transfer it to other settings. Few research studies have employed self-control training, but early indications are that this is the best way both of improving perfor-mance through use of a specific strategy and also of transferring the training to appropriate new situations. Self-control training uses instruction, practice, feedback, practice, more feedback, and more practice until the strategy becomes automatic. Students remember not what they hear or see but what they do (Craik and Tulving, 1975). Instead of merely telling students what to do, we must put them to work.

Variables in Studying

Self-control training is successful only if certain basic considerations are kept in mind. Brown, Campione, and Day (1981) have summarized a tetrahedral model of learning, in which studying is seen as a complex interaction among four factors: the cognitive and affective characteristics of learners, the nature of the materials being studied, the critical task that is the purpose of studying, and the learning strategies being used. We will look briefly at three of these here.

Characteristics of Learners. Like good drivers, effective students remain constantly in charge of their situation and respond to the varying nature and degree of the demands placed on them as they proceed. For a start, good students study long enough to make the effort pay off. They use their monitoring skills first to recognize what they know and do not know, then to process material in such a way as to understand, store, and make it available for eventual retrieval. That is, they use self-regulatory skills to make best use of their cognitive skills. If they have shortcomings, they adapt techniques and cope with their limitations. If, for instance, they frequently misspell words or make arithmetic errors, they consciously develop a selective suspicion toward their spelling of words and their calculations. Sometimes, they rehearse spelling rules and multiplication tables. The point is to minimize a weakness. Some highly motivated students have succeeded in turning such weaknesses into strengths. As learner characteristics pertain to note-taking, students with illegible cursive writing could learn to print their notes, develop abbreviations for frequently used terms, and write more carefully. Since these student experts are generally well aware of their background knowledge, special aptitudes, and high motivation, they employ these strengths as needed to meet the demands of the critical task (Baker and Brown, in press). In learning, excellent students use everything they can about their knowledge of the critical task, their general background in the area, and their expertise in strategies. This integration of past experience and present endeavor greatly increases learning (R. C. Anderson and others, 1977).

Nature of the Materials Being Studied. Despite the poor writing in some textbooks, excellent students recognize that texts tend to display logical structures both in their form and in their content. Students who process texts thoroughly notice summaries, headings and subheadings, relationship signals, and statements emphasizing certain material as important. They know typical patterns of paragraph development, such as generalization-example, comparison, classification, cause-effect, part-whole, chronological sequence, definition, and analysis. Not surprisingly, identification of these features greatly assists in learning (Shimmerlik, 1978; Walker and Meyer, 1980). Lectures are likely to have at least something of an organization around a few main ideas. Listening for the organization can help, as can previous reading of parallel material in the text.

The Learning Strategies Being Used. Excellent students consciously depend on both their cognitive and their metacognitive skills to respond to the demands of the critical task. They concentrate on the task, blocking out distractions. In reading, they vary the rate of study, to assure comprehension. Harder material gets more time and special processing. They emphasize material important to the critical task. In the absence of specific knowledge about a task, they identify and spend extra time on main ideas.

Further, they deliberately seek to learn the material. Experts describe learning in terms like *levels of processing* (R. C. Anderson, 1970, 1972; Craik and Lockhart, 1972), *encoding specificity* (Tulving and Thomson, 1973), and *spread of encoding* (Craik and Tulving, 1975). The point of these theories can be combined by students in actual practice, as follows: A verbal stimulus can be elaborated by a context of further structural, phonemic, and semantic encodings. In this elaboration, semantic processing is particularly valuable for recognizing and recalling. They also gain by anticipating what will be on a test and by rehearsing the retrieval, using cues that they can expect to encounter in the test. As T. H. Anderson and Armbruster (in press) say, learners will study effectively if they "process the right information in the right way, where *right information* is defined with respect to the criterion task, and *right way* connotes a relatively deep or meaningful involvement with the text."

In addition, excellent students monitor on-going activities to assure that they are comprehending. They take action to remediate failures in reading comprehension. (Some of these steps seem obvious, but they are not always obvious to students who need help.) That is, they slow down. They concentrate on the task, minimizing distractions. They reread the difficult materials. They refer back to preceding material in the text. They check their class notes. They look ahead in the text. They search their memory for related material already learned. They consult a dictionary or reference work, a classmate, their instructor, or another authority. Since these resources are not always immediately available, they note their questions in writing and include page numbers, to assure that they do not forget to ask them or that they do not forget what caused the puzzlement. They resume reading, attempting to see the difficult point as part of the whole in which it is embedded. Sometimes, they decide that the puzzle is not worth solving, especially if the point at issue has little bearing on the critical task or on personal interest.

Excellent students reconsider their strategies of thinking about the material, seeking a more effective way to open the locked box. Finally, they even know when to stop studying and take a break, eat, exercise, or sleep. They organize their time to vary the routine, knowing how to balance variety against perseverance.

Turning Insights into Programs

As a result of these valuable insights gathered from recent research, we now know at least some of the principles involved in training students to learn effectively. Students should be taught the importance of the cognitive and affective characteristics that they bring to the task, the nature of the materials, and the various study strategies that are available. But, how easily can we expect to teach it? In this case, common experience is supported by the limited research. Only with extensive training will students be able to use what we teach. They did not acquire their attitudes, skills, and habits overnight, and all our sincerity, authority, and caring will not make them change overnight. For a detailed training program involving complex interaction of academic and technical activities, see Dansereau and others (1979).

It is instructive here to compare a change in students' learning of study skills to acquisition of a second language. Both processes involve a number of features that one brings to the situation of learning, and both require fundamental changes in attitudes, skills, and habits. Studies indicate that these changes are not easy even when one uses metacognitive resources. Indeed, change is said to be limited to new features of learning different from those already known—it is difficult to replace old thinking and habits with new—and to features that are relatively easy to keep in mind for self-monitoring—anything long and complicated will not easily be remembered, much less applied (Krashen, 1977).

If we keep these restrictions on learning in mind, we will not ask students to acquire a whole new system of reading, note-taking, or problem solving from two easy lectures or from a handout that they are to take home, decipher, and apply as a habit. For any skill that we truly desire to teach, not simply to cover, we must determine its essential elements; divide the instruction into sections, each of which can be learned at one sitting; direct students in practicing the subroutines; and follow initial instruction with distributed practice. That is, we must find each individual's instructional level and train until the individual reaches that level.

Note-Taking

Let us consider note-taking in light of metacognition and the four basic variables involved in training students. As already noted, research on the effectiveness of note-taking is divided. Here, we will consider the implications of studies in which note-taking was found to be effective.

Three Theories of Note-Taking. Various researchers, using the terminology of Rothkopf (1970), regard note-taking as *mathemagenic activity*—that is, overt activity that in some way influences the outcome of learning. Peper and Mayer (1978) mention three possible explanations for the mathemagenic character of note-taking. The attention theory holds that taking notes increases a subject's overall attention and orientation to the new material. The effort theory relies on the fact that note-taking requires more effort and deeper encoding of the material than mere reading does. Finally, the generative theory notices that subjects who take notes must paraphrase, organize, and make sense of material; they are thus induced to integrate new information with their own experience.

All these theories require that students take notes thoughtfully! However, numerous studies report that note-takers performed no better on tests than students who only read. Thus, it stands to reason that note-taking works only if the student does. To adopt the terms of the three theories just mentioned, students who want to learn something would do well to focus their attention, put forth some effort, and generate some connections between new material and their own experience.

Two reasons make these theories worth our notice here. In the first place, students who rely on magic, not sound principles of note-taking, are not necessarily lazy; sometimes, they simply do not know how to take useful notes. This leads us to the second reason why these theories deserve our attention: Educators must devise training programs to help students learn how to take notes that accomplish their intended purpose. The student will have to be flexible in learning. This is by no means obvious to every student, so it will have to be taught. Flexibility in note-taking should become as widely recommended as flexibility in reading rate already is. Two systems with promise, mapping and networking, have been described by T. H. Anderson (1979) and Dansereau and others (1979), respectively.

Other Studies of Note-Taking. Research has produced some other insights into the note-taking process. Shimmerlik and Nolan (1976) found that students who reorganized material while taking notes, rather than recording it in the author's organization, performed better on a free-recall test. This implies that reorganizing material for oneself requires processing that is good preparation for an essay test.

Bretzing and Kulhavy (1979) assigned students to one of four groups, each of which used different types of note-taking (summaries of individual pages, paraphrase of main ideas, verbatim notes from the text, or letter searching—recording individual, capitalized words), or to a control group that took no notes. The students were to write a short sentence in answer to questions, which "were of a substantive, integrative nature, requiring a combination of facts from the passage, and not a simple, verbatim answer" (Bretzing and Kulhavy, 1979, p. 148). Students who summarized and paraphrased showed approximately the same performance, which was better than that of the control and verbatim groups, who in turn outperformed the letter searchers. The authors attributed the results to differences in depth of processing of the material. In addition, T. H. Anderson and Armbruster (in press) point out that the summarizers and paraphrasers enjoyed the advantage of encoding material in a form compatible with the requirements of the criterion task.

Research conducted by Schultz and Di Vesta (1972) to determine the effect on recall of various organizations of text disclosed that organized material was easier to recall than random material. But, the authors were struck by the discovery that students tended to exhibit a preferred strategy of clustering. That is, many of them favored a certain organization of the material, even when the passage was organized in a different way. The authors speculate that the preference might lie in the "experience in the culture" (Schultz and Di Vesta, 1972, p. 251). Whether they are right or not, their study encourages us to investigate the organizational patterns that students are using at the time when we meet them.

Fisher and Harris (1973) found that students who took their own notes and reviewed them outperformed students in four other groups that combined note-taking and review in different ways. They also found that subjects' performance on the free-recall and objective tests administered immediately after the lecture and on the posttest administered three weeks later was not related to the subjects' liking for taking notes. If these results can be generalized to all students, then we can ask our students to give the training program an honest try. Even if they are not predisposed to enjoy taking notes, they can probably benefit from it. For some people, note-taking could become an acquired taste.

Additional evidence of the importance of intentional encoding of material comes from Orlando (1980). In that study, students either took notes to be studied later or took notes to help them remember. On both immediate and delayed-recall tests, the group that took notes to help them remember recalled more, probably because they processed the material more meaningfully and purposefully.

Applications for Educators

Up to this point, we have dwelt on what students should do. The implications for educators have been largely unstated. Now, it is appropriate to be explicit: We need to make best use of our own cognitive and meta-cognitive strengths, to examine the nature of our critical task (training students to learn for themselves), to inquire into the nature of the material itself (the students and what they study), and to employ the strategies appropriate to accomplishing the task.

A Starting Point. The first thing that some of us have to do is to distinguish between authoritative advice and personal quirks. Since authority is scarce, we are well advised when we first meet our students to spend more time in getting to know them than in plying them with advice. If we go to a physician with a pain, we expect to be questioned extensively about our personal and family history and about all the circumstances connected with the pain. If the doctor heard only that we had a headache and prescribed medication on that basis alone, we doubt that the medicine would help; we might even suspect that it could cause harm. Reasonably, we expect diagnosis to precede treatment.

For the same reasons, students deserve to be examined before they are advised. Here are three diagnostic strategies: analysis of some actual notes taken by students during lectures or reading, analysis of students' notes on a specimen lecture or sample text, and student interviews.

Analysis of some actual notes taken by students during lectures or readings, can help the instructor to learn much, whether the instructor knows the lectures and readings at first hand or not. The question to ask is this: What do the notes represent to the note-taker? Neat notes are easier to read than sloppy ones, but it is not reasonable to judge students on neatness. Still, notes that are incomprehensible for any reason defeat the purpose of note-taking. It is more important to ask questions such as these: Have the students understood the lecture or the material? Have they recognized its main points, details, and relationships? Have they formed a representation of it in memory? Have they integrated it with their own experience? Have they anticipated the ways in which they will have to retrieve it for a teacher? Clearly, some notes are more systematic, practical, and valuable than others, and we should not hesitate to offer alternatives for students to consider, as long as the alternatives take into account the principles that we have been discussing. As an alternative, students can take notes on a specimen lecture, delivered in person or via audio or video recording. A sample text can serve the same purpose. Analysis of students' notes would be conducted as just described.

Finally, students can be interviewed. Here is a list of some issues involved in the simple business of note-taking.

1. *Attitudes*

   Belief in oneself: confidence
   Trying to succeed: effort
   Trying to improve: bettering
   Faith in the academic situation: trust
   Willingness to receive help: accepting
   Willingness to seek help: seeking
   Observation of oneself in action: self-monitoring
   Aiming for fullness of knowledge: mastering
   Seeking to fulfill personal goals: self-satisfaction
   Pleasing the grade-giver: task specification

2. *General Skills*

   Managing time
   Listening for structure in lectures
   Reading for structure in text
   Concentrating
   Relating material to course needs
   Relating material to personal needs
   Adapting studying to the task
      Memorizing
      Solving problems
      Organizing
      Discriminating concepts presented in the material
      Composing, writing
      Researching
   Self-monitoring
   Self-testing
   Rehearsing

3. *Note-Taking Skills*

a. For a lecture:
What to listen for
When to write
How to write concisely
How to organize
How to distinguish main points from details
How to spot the lecturer's organization
When to edit the notes after lecture
How to use the notes

b. For a textbook:
What to mark
How much to mark
How to use margins
How to use separate sheets
What form to use for the notes
How to spot the text's organization
How to fit lecture and text together
How to be sure that one knows the material

c. Using notes:
When to memorize
How to memorize
How to adapt to the type of study called for

4. *Habits*

Having needed materials
Being in the right place at the right time
Working enough
Using the best methods available
Targeting study to the task
Self-monitoring
Seeking feedback
Self-testing
Reviewing
Seeking something for oneself

Student interviews should address these issues. Using our cognitive and metacognitive skills, we should analyze what the student says, keeping alert to failures of communication on either person's part and being aware of the many ways in which a student's problem can manifest itself first as poor notes.

Conclusion

From our consideration of note-taking as it relates to several fundamental concepts involved in learning, it becomes clear that much of our responsibility as educators lies in training students thoroughly, step by step and skill by skill, to take responsibility for their own education. Note-taking is not just one technique preferred by the teachers; rather, it is a range of methods for meaningful processing that students can learn. Study skills, as many learning activities are called, are intimately related to what we know about ourselves. When we as educators assist students to see themselves in relation to the materials, demands, and strategies of their learning, we make a sizable contribution to their lives.

References

Anderson, R. C. "Control of Student Mediating Processes During Verbal Learning and Instruction." *Review of Educational Research,* 1970, *40* (3), 349–369.

Anderson, R. C. "How to Construct Achievement Tests to Assess Comprehension." *Review of Educational Research,* 1972, *42* (2), 145–170.

Anderson, R. C., and others. "Frameworks for Comprehending Discourse." *American Educational Research Journal,* 1977, *14* (4), 367–381.

Anderson, T. H. "Study Skills and Learning Strategies." In H. F. O'Neil and C. D. Spielberger (Eds.), *Cognitive and Affective Learning Strategies.* New York: Academic Press, 1979.

Anderson, T. H., and Armbruster, B. B. "Studying," In D. Pearson (Ed.), *Handbook on Research in Reading.* New York: Longman, in press.

Baker, L., and Brown, A. L. "Metacognitive Skills of Reading." In D. Pearson (Ed.), *Handbook of Reading Research.* New York: Longman, in press.

Bretzing, B. H., and Kulhavy, R. W. "Note-Taking and Depth of Processing." *Contemporary Educational Psychology,* 1979, *4,* 145–153.

Brown, A. L., Campione, J. C., and Day, J. D. "Learning to Learn: On Training Students to Learn from Texts." *Educational Researcher,* 1981, *10,* 14–21.

Carrier, C. A., and Titus, A. "The Effects of Note-Taking: A Review of Studies." *Contemporary Educational Psychology,* 1979, *4,* 299–314.

Craik, F. I. M., and Lockhart, R. S. "Levels of Processing: A Framework for Memory Research." *Journal of Verbal Learning and Verbal Behavior,* 1972, *11,* 671–684.

Craik, F. I. M., and Tulving, E. "Depth of Processing and the Retention of Words in Episodic Memory." *Journal of Educational Psychology,* 1975, *104* (3), 268–294.

Dansereau, D. F., and others. "Evaluation of a Learning Strategy System." In H. F. O'Neil, Jr. and C. D. Spielberger (Eds.), *Cognitive and Affective Learning Strategies.* New York: Academic Press, 1979.

Fisher, J. L., and Harris, M. B. "Effect of Note-Taking and Review on Recall." *Journal of Educational Psychology,* 1973, *65* (3), 321–325.

Flavell, J. H. "Metacognitive Development." In J. M. Scandura and C. J. Brainerd (Eds.), *Structural/Process Theories of Complex Human Behavior.* Alphen, the Netherlands: Sijthoff and Noordhoff, 1978.

Krashen, S. D. "Some Issues Relating to the Monitor Model." In H. D. Brown, C. A. Yorio, and R. H. Crymes (Eds.), *Teaching and Learning English as a Second Language: Trends in Research and Practice.* Washington, D. C.: Teachers of English to Speakers of Other Languages, 1977.

Marshall, J. C., and Morton, J. "On the Mechanics of EMMA." In A. Sinclair, R. J. Jarvella, and W. J. M. Levelt (Eds.), *The Child's Conception of Language.* Berlin: Springer-Verlag, 1978.

Michaels, J. W. "Classroom Reward Structures and Academic Performance." *Review of Educational Research,* 1977, *47* (1), 87–98.

Orlando, V. "A Comparison of Note-Taking Strategies While Studying from Text." In M. Kamil and A. Moe (Eds.), *Perspectives on Reading Research and Instruction; Twenty-Ninth Yearbook of the National Reading Conference.* Washington, D. C.: National Reading Conference, 1980.

Peper, R. J., and Mayer, R. E. "Note-Taking as a Generative Activity," *Journal of Educational Psychology,* 1978, *70* (4), 514–522.

Rothkopf, E. Z. "The Concept of Mathemagenic Activities." *Review of Educational Research,* 1970, *40*, 325–336.

Schultz, C. B., and Di Vesta, F. J. "Effects of Passage Organization and Note-Taking on the Selection of Clustering Strategies and on Recall of Textual Materials." *Journal of Educational Psychology,* 1972, *63* (3), 244–252.

Shimmerlik, S. M. "Organization Theory and Memory for Prose: A Review of the Literature." *Review of Educational Research,* 1978, *48* (1), 103–120.

Shimmerlik, S. M., and Nolan, J. D. "Reorganization and the Recall of Prose." *Journal of Educational Psychology,* 1976, *68* (6), 779–786.

Tulving, E., and Thomson, D. M. "Encoding Specificity and Retrieval Processes in Episodic Memory." *Psychological Review,* 1973, *80* (5), 352–373.

Walker, C. H., and Meyer, B. J. F. "Integrating Information from Text: An Evaluation of Current Theories." *Review of Educational Research,* 1980, *50* (3), 421–437.

John Whitney Milton is director of the Expanded Encounter with Learning Program and assistant dean of students at the University of Illinois, Urbana-Champaign. Since 1971 he has developed and refined a comprehensive program for training tutors and peer counselors to help students learn for themselves.

Viewing reading comprehension as analytical reasoning provides
useful insights into design of materials and classroom procedures
that improve skill in comprehension.

Analytical Reasoning and Reading Comprehension

Arthur Whimbey
John Glade

Farr (1971) pointed out that, from the very first reading test—the Kansas Silent Reading Test of 1916—through current instruments like the California Achievement Test, questions appearing in tests of reading comprehension bear a strong similarity to questions on standard verbal intelligence tests. Fry (1972) advised teachers that intelligence is the chief factor in reading comprehension. Recent studies on the mental activities of intelligence and analytical reasoning bear these suggestions out, shedding an interesting light on the nature and teaching of comprehension processes.

The Mental Activities of Analytical Reasoning

Here is a verbal analogy question of the type found on many IQ and academic aptitude tests, such as the SAT (Whimbey and Lochhead, 1981):

Research reported here was partially supported by grant #G008005201 from the Fund for the Improvement of Postsecondary Education.

A. S. Algier, K. W. Algier (Eds.). *New Directions for College Learning Assistance: Improving Reading and Study Skills,* no. 8. San Francisco: Jossey-Bass, June 1982

Arm is to wrist as _____ is to _____ .
A. leg : foot   B. thigh : ankle
C. leg : ankle   D. leg : knee

Solving this problem requires subjects to take a series of careful mental steps. A skilled thinker may begin by examining the relationship between arm and wrist, visualizing an arm and noting that the wrist is the joint at one end. Then, he might examine each alternative in the same way, until he found that C formed the best parallel. Unskilled thinkers sometimes pick alternative B, because they do not consider that thigh means not the entire leg but only the upper leg. Sometimes, they pick alternative A, because the wrist is at the end of the arm, and the foot is at the end of the leg. They do not work in careful steps, examining the anatomical relationships developed by the alternatives to find the closest parallel. Researchers such as Bloom and Broder (1950) have observed that analyses of information by students with low IQ scores tend to lack sufficient detail and precision for the responses or answers required.

Here is another IQ test question, which requires subjects to follow somewhat complex directions (Whimbey and Lochhead, 1981). Questions of this type are often found on reading comprehension tests.

Cross out the letter after the letter in the word *pardon* which is in the same position in the word as it is in the alphabet.

Analyzing and interpreting this statement involves the same step-by-step process used in comprehending Internal Revenue Service forms or textbooks in sciences like chemistry and physics. One successful student read and thought aloud as follows: "Cross out the letter after the letter (I'm confused, but I think I have to cross out a letter) in the word (cross out a letter in some word) *pardon* (so *pardon* must be the word)." The student continued and noticed that *d* was in the same position in *pardon* as it is in the alphabet. When he went back to reread the first part, which had been initially confusing, he saw that the letter after the *d,* namely the *o,* had to be crossed out.

Unsuccessful students miss steps and lose information. They often cross out the *d* in pardon, having lost "the letter after the letter." Occasionally, their misinterpretation goes further and they cross out the *d* in *word.*

Accurate, Step-by-Step Thinking in Reading

The following reading selection and three comprehension questions (Whimbey, 1982) illustrate how careful, step-by-step thinking is used in comprehending and reaching conclusions with standard textbook prose.

Infectious diseases are the only ones that can be transmitted. They may be spread by infected animals, infected people, or contaminated substances, such as food and water. Infectious diseases that can be transmitted to humans from infected animals are known as zoonoses. Zoonoses may be transmitted by carriers, such as insects; by the bite of an infected animal; by direct contact with an infected animal or its excretions; or by eating animal products.

1. Zoonoses are:
   a. Insects that carry diseases.
   b. Infected animals that transmit infectious diseases to humans.
   c. Infectious diseases that man gets from animals.
   d. Carriers that transmit infectious diseases.

2. In the space before each title in column I, write the letter of the correct description from column II.

	I	II
_____	*Transmission of Infectious Diseases*	a. Too narrow
_____	*Types and Mechanisms of Diseases*	b. Too broad
_____	*How Zoonoses Are Transmitted*	c. Comprehensive title

3. The passage implies that:
   a. Noninfectious diseases can be transmitted by animals.
   b. Noninfectious diseases can be transmitted by sick people.
   c. Noninfectious diseases cannot be transmitted by sick people.

Question One requires careful reading in order to understand the information contained in the third sentence. An unsuccessful student who read the sentence inaccurately based his answer on the last six words of the sentence, namely "infected animals are known as zoonoses." Consequently, he chose alternative B: "Zoonoses are infected animals."

Question Two requires reading each title carefully to determine the topics that it includes, then comparing these topics to the topics covered in the reading selection. This is a step-by-step process, which resembles the precise interpretations and comparisons required for the previous analogy problem. When we asked a good reader to exlain his reasoning in answering this question, he said that the title *Types and Mechanisms of Diseases* was too broad, because a selection that bore that title would have to include other diseases besides infectious ones as well as a description of mechanisms. He judged the title *How Zoonoses Are Transmitted* to be too narrow, because the selection discusses infectious diseases other than zoonoses. The title *Transmission of Infectious Diseases* covers all the topics addressed in the selection, so he picked it as the comprehensive title.

Question Three requires the student to go beyond the information that is given and decide what implication can be drawn from the selection. A careful reader might read the three answer alternatives and note that two say "Noninfectious diseases can be transmitted," while the third ssays "Noninfectious diseases cannot be transmitted." He might then either remember or go back and see that the selection says "Infectious diseases are the only ones that can be transmitted." The word *only* in this statement implies alternative C: Noninfectious diseases cannot be transmitted.

Teaching Accurate, Step-by-Step Thinking

One approach to helping students improve their analytical skill uses a series of reading exercises requiring an increasing number of steps. Reading teachers in effect do this when they give students practice with exercises at increasingly higher grade levels. To supplement this regular practice, a set of sixty exercises has been developed to teach students to comprehend increasingly complex written descriptions of serial order. Here are three representative exercises from near the beginning, middle, and end of the set (Whimbey, 1982).

1. Atlanta has a larger population than Birmingham but a smaller population than Chicago. Write the names of the three cities in order on the diagram.

larger

smaller

2. Lake Superior in the United States is the world's largest lake, with the exception of the Caspian Sea, which was mistaken to be a sea by the ancient Romans but is considered to be a lake by modern geographers, because it is landlocked. Skipping over lakes Aral and Victoria, the next largest lake is also in the U.S., Lake Huron. The African Lake Victoria is larger than the Russian Lake Aral. Write the names of the five lakes in order by size on a diagram.

3. William Harvey, the Englishman who published the first description of the blood's circulation, was born between Marcello Malpighi, a Bologna professor who was younger than Harvey and who extended Harvey's theory by using a microscope to show that blood passed from the arteries to the smaller veins, and Galileo, the astronomer who introduced the microscope to science. Thomas Sydenham, a London physician born

between these two pioneers of research on circulation, is sometimes called the founder of modern clinical medicine because of his precise description of diseases like malaria and smallpox, whereas Hermann Boerhaave, a Dutch physician born after the Bologna professor mentioned earlier, was considered the greatest medical professor of his day, owing to his use of the clinical method on teaching and research. Athanasius Kircher—born before Anton van Leeuwenhoek, who made a microscope that magnified objects 270 times, wrote the first complete description of red blood cells, and was the first person to see bacteria, but after "the greatest medical professor of his day"—theorized from his research with the microscope that bacteria caused disease and decay, although this was not confirmed for two hundred years. Write the names of the seven researchers in order of date of birth on a diagram.

Students who worked through the entire set of sixty exercises showed improved skill in comprehending complex descriptions of order in size, chronology, and spatial position. They also reported feeling that they had learned to read more precisely and analytically in textbooks and on reading tests. These feelings were supported by improved scores on the Iowa Silent Reading Test.

Vocalized Thinking

A second approach that is being used increasingly for improving analytical reading and reasoning is to have students think aloud or to explain their reasoning as they answer comprehension questions. This approach results from a recognition that the mental activities of analysis and comprehension are generally carried on inside the head, where they are hidden from view, which makes them difficult to teach and learn (Whimbey, 1979).

Benjamin Bloom was one of the first educators to recognize the problem. In a study conducted by Bloom and Broder (1950), unsuccessful students worked in small groups with a tutor, taking turns reading information and thinking aloud as they answered questions. Students found that by thinking aloud they became more aware of gaps and inadequacies in their reading and reasoning. Bloom and Broder reported that students learned to read with greater care and to reason more actively and accurately. These students also showed a statistically significant gain on the University of Chicago's comprehensive examination, which required reading information from various academic disciplines to answer questions.

An application of the discussion-oriented approach with younger students is seen in a program called *Think* (1975). In this program, the teacher works with a group of five students, while the remainder of the class does individualized work, sometimes under the supervision of a paraprofessional. Students follow a passage that is being read aloud. Then, they answer questions that involve comprehension, which require them to form analogies, recognize trends, or analyze other relationships. Subsequently, each student is asked not only to give his answer but also to explain it, and discussion between students is encouraged when answers differ. In a study by one school administrator (Besteiro, 1980), below-average junior high students who used *Think* achieved a mean gain on the SRA Achievement Series: Reading that was five times their expected gain. In another district, an evaluator (Harckham, 1979) conducted a longitudinal study assessing the effectiveness of continued use of the program by the same students over three successive school years. Below-average students using *Think* in their seventh, eighth, and ninth grades achieved mean gains on the Iowa subtests of vocabulary and comprehension two and one-half times their expected gains for that time period, based on the historical regression technique suggested by the New York State Education Department.

Another variation of the discussion-oriented approach is used by project SOAR at Xavier University (New Orleans), a traditionally black institution (Whimbey and others, 1980). Project SOAR (Stress On Analytical Reasoning) is a five-week prefreshman summer program serving approximately 125 students per summer, who are divided into five groups of twenty-five. To improve reading and reasoning skill, students work in pairs, alternating as problem solver and listener to solve analogy and word problems of the types shown earlier. The problem solver does all his thinking and reasoning aloud, while the listener pays close attention to ensure that the problem solver proceeds in an accurate, step-by-step manner. On reading selections as long as the zoonoses piece discussed earlier, students read and answer the questions independently, then compare answers with their partners and discuss and explain their reasoning where answers differ. When all partners agree, the instructor asks various students for their answers and again encourages discussion on any differences. SOAR has been used for several summers at Xavier, and each time, students register an average gain of roughly one and a half years on the Nelson-Denny Reading Test and one hundred points on the SAT.

Correcting Speed-Reading Misconceptions

Viewing good comprehension of difficult material as analytical reasoning has called some of the practices recommended by speed-reading courses into question. Moreover, many students with weak comprehension skill have misconceptions about good reading habits, which they have acquired from taking or hearing about speed-reading courses. At Xavier University, Clark College, and other institutions where comprehension is taught as analytical reasoning, instructors have found it worthwhile to spend some class time discussing and dispelling these misconceptions. Here is a brief summary of their advice.

Misconception 1: Don't subvocalize. Be a totally visual reader. This misconception stems from a concern with speeding up the reading process. However, many good readers, such as college professors, report that they regularly subvocalize while reading. It seems to improve their comprehension without appreciably reducing their speed. People differ in the degree to which they find subvocalizing useful. Therefore, students should be told to subvocalize freely whenever it improves their ability to understand what they are reading.

Misconception 2: Don't be a word-by-word reader. Read several words per fixation. Dechant (1962) pointed out that, while teachers have urged children to read two and three words per fixation, the best studies show that even college students rarely read more than one word per fixation. The assumption that people could recognize two- and three-word units was based on misinterpretations of tachistoscopic research that confused one-shot, tachistoscopic reading with continuous, normal reading. Dechant emphasized that the limiting factor in recognition is not the eye but the mind's ability to process and organize incoming material.

Misconception 3: Make your eyes read in thought groups. This misconception is closely related to the previous one. Since good readers basically read one word at a time, they obviously do not read in thought groups. Naturally, in reading, one groups words together mentally. Verbs and prepositions link nouns with other nouns, and so on. However, we cannot read in thought groups in the sense that we can focus visually on groups of words that form thoughts. Indeed, this is logically impossible. It is impossible to know which words form a thought group before one reads the words.

Misconception 4: Don't regress or reread. Speed reading experts instruct students never to regress or reread a section of material, even if they feel that they have not understood it well. Rereading is said to be a bad reading habit and totally unproductive. Instead, students are told to forge ahead and that their understanding will be clarified as they read on. However, studies show that good readers do not follow this advice. With textbooks and other complicated material, they must frequently reread whole sentences and paragraphs to get the full meaning.

Conclusion. Research on reasoning has revealed that good problem solvers subvocalize as they read and think, work in small units, take pains not to misread even one word, and often reread and reconsider information. In general, their approach contradicts much of the advice publicized by speed-reading experts.

Teaching Analytical Thinking in All Classes

The responsibility for teaching students to analyze and comprehend written material has generally been placed upon the reading teacher. But while the reading teacher can play a central role in this training, research like Frankenstein's (1979) indicates that the greatest gains are obtained when teachers in all classes reinforce analytical thinking. In Frankenstein's program, which is now being used in forty-two schools in Israel, whenever a student gives an incorrect answer, whether in history, chemistry, or Bible class, the instructor asks him to explain how he arrived at the answer. This can mean going back to the text to read and interpret pertinent sections. It can also mean detailing the operations and logic used in reaching the answer. Frankenstein's approach is being adopted by an increasing number of teachers in America. As teachers from the first grade through college begin to tell students to "Be accurate" and "Explain how you obtained that answer," it will be exciting to see how effectively and efficiently the comprehension skills of students can be improved.

References

Besteiro, R. A. *An Evaluation of Think and Intuitive Math.* Brownsville, Tex.: Brownsville Independent School District, 1980.

Bloom, B. S., and Broder, L. *Problem-Solving Processes of College Students.* Chicago: University of Chicago Press, 1950.

Dechant, E. "Misinterpretations of Theory and/or Research Lead to Errors in Practice." In E. P. Bleismer and R. C. Staiger (Eds.), *Problems, Programs, and Projects in College-Adult Reading; Eleventh Yearbook of the National Reading Conference.* Milwaukee, Wisc.: National Reading Conference, 1962 (ED 176 250).

Farr, R. "Measuring Reading Comprehension: An Historical Perspective." In F. P. Greene (Ed.), *Reading: The Right to Participate; Twentieth Yearbook of the National Reading Conference.* Milwaukee, Wisc.: National Reading Conference, 1971 (ED 176 246).

Frankenstein, C. *They Think Again: Restoring Cognitive Abilities Through Teaching.* New York: Van Nostrand Reinhold, 1979.

Fry, E. *Reading Instruction for Classroom and Clinic.* New York: McGraw-Hill, 1972.

Harckham, L. *An Evaluation of Think: A Language Arts Developmental Reading Program.* New Rochelle, N. Y.: Isaac E. Young Junior High School, 1979.

Think. Stamford, Conn.: Innovative Sciences, 1975.

Whimbey, A. *Intelligence Can Be Taught.* New York: Dutton, 1979.

Whimbey, A. *Analytical Reading.* Stamford, Conn. Innovative Sciences, 1982.

Whimbey A., Carmichael, J. W., Jones, L., and Hunter, J. "Teaching Critical Reading and Analytical Reasoning in Project SOAR." *Journal of Reading,* 1980, *24,* 5–10.

Whimbey, A., and Lochhead, J. *Problem Solving and Comprehension: A Short Course in Analytical Reasoning.* Philadelphia: Franklin Institute Press, 1981.

Arthur Whimbey is resident scholar in the Department of Reading, Clark College (Atlanta, Georgia). A member of the editorial board for Problem Solving: A Monthly Newsletter *and* Human Intelligence: International Newsletter, *he has published articles in numerous journals.*

John J. Glade is director of research and design, ISI THINK, Inc. (Stamford, Connecticut). He currently conducts seminars on cognitive skills-based curriculum design and teaching strategies.

Study systems that assist students in organizing, reducing, and storing information are available. Content area instructors should promote use of such systems.

Coping with College Textbooks: A Study System

Ann S. Algier

Administrators and faculty in higher education are, or should be, concerned by the fact that students with less than adequate reading skills are enrolling in colleges and universities. Furthermore, nationwide studies disclose that there are wide disparities between students' reading abilities and the levels expected for textbook comprehension. Fortunately, systems based on sound principles of learning have been designed to help students gain control of the subject matter in textbooks. Content area instructors need to promote the use of these systems, and students need to acquire an awareness of how and why they are effective.

In this regard, students need to know three things: what to extract from textbooks, how to extract essential elements from vast amounts of information, and how to store and retrieve these elements for examinations. Such skills are critically needed beyond graduation, according to a study by the National Assessment of Educational Progress (*Reading, Thinking, and Writing*, 1981), which maintains that, in a world overloaded with information, the advantage will go to individuals who have skills in reducing and interpreting data. According to this study, fewer people seem to be reading efficiently, although this is a time when more information must be distilled and mastered faster than ever before in history.

A. S. Algier, K. W. Algier (Eds.). *New Directions for College Learning Assistance: Reading and Study Skills*, no. 8. San Francisco: Jossey-Bass, June 1982

Understanding Structure

Understanding the basic structure of textbook chapters facilitates extraction of essential elements. Recent studies disclosed that one effective strategy is to identify the author's organizational pattern or schema. Students who can identify an author's organizational schema can comprehend and recall more information than students who cannot (Meyer and Freedle, 1979). Paragraph headings and titles add to the reader's comprehension by helping to establish the author's framework. Doctorow and others (1978) found that headings can serve as retrieval cues to aid students in activating experiential background for association with new material.

Survey Techniques. For many years, reading practitioners have been teaching students to use Francis Robinson's SQR3 method to preview or survey a text, thereby making the author's schema more understandable. Unfortunately, students have not been asked to practice this method. Students need to apply the survey method in a variety of settings, adapting the formula to fit various discourse patterns. Figure 1 presents a version of Robinson's survey method modified for textbook study. Students who master the flowchart adaptation will respond actively, which will enhance their concentration and comprehension.

A preliminary survey of the entire textbook should precede a chapter analysis. Students can be directed to divide a sheet of paper into a sufficient number of squares to accommodate each chapter. In this initial reconnaissance of the textbook, students are asked to write each chapter heading, one to a square. Then, they are told to skim each chapter for the important words. In many cases, the important words will be found in the summary or conclusion sections and in boldface type or italics within the text itself. The key words—that is, the concepts—should be written in the square that represents the chapter.

Concept Control. Obviously, concept knowledge is basic to understanding the text. Students need to master the major concepts before tackling an assignment, especially if they have no prior knowledge of the subject. While current research demonstrates the importance of knowledge of text structure, it is also clear that word knowledge is requisite for reading comprehension. People who are deficient in vocabulary skills are probably poor readers (Mandler and Johnson, 1977). If a totally new vocabulary word is introduced without explanation or definition, the student may encounter a learning block. The consequent temporary hiatus in understanding induces anxiety even in good students. Preventing such situations is justification enough for surveying a textbook assignment before trying to read it through or before listening to a lecture on the subject. Students need to be aware that they must be familiar with new concepts before they read the assignment. And, once the student has become conscious of words in boldface type and italics and has learned to use the glossary (if one is

Figure 1. Textbook Chapter Study System: An Aid to Comprehension

Directions: Use Your Hands! Direct your eyes to paragraph headings, italicized expressions, graphics and captions.

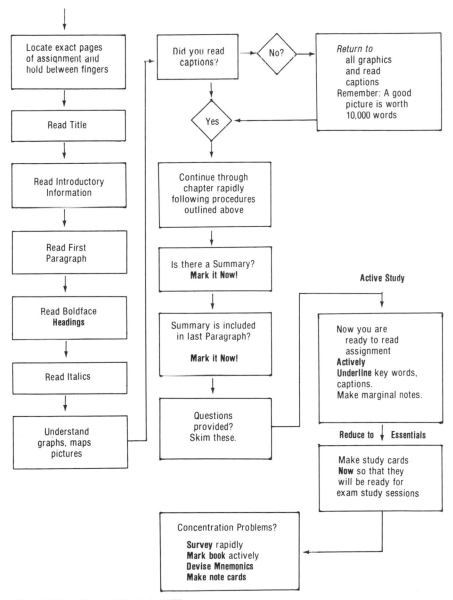

provided), the entire business of studying becomes more meaningful and less exasperating.

Demonstrating Survey Techniques. After students become familiar with the format of the textbook, instructors should lead them through a survey of the first chapter, explaining how and why the technique works. Numerous studies have demonstrated that rapid survey of a chapter leads to increased comprehension. Why? A quick overview stimulates interest, which in turn aids concentration. Because man is by nature a curious animal, he feels a need to know, and this natural curiosity provides motivation to study. Furthermore, most students are reluctant to settle down to study, and they benefit from a mental warm-up in much the same way that runners benefit from stretching exercises; a chapter preview provides such a warm-up.

The Importance of Graphics. The interpretation of charts, maps, diagrams, graphs, and other illustrations has been neglected. Too often, students think that illustrations are included simply to fill space or to make the book more attractive. They need to be made conscious of the fact that information reduced to diagrammatic form can be learned more easily. Frequently, a great deal of data can be summarized in a single graphic. There is evidence to support the view that pictures and other graphics enhance comprehension. Just as with titles and paragraph headings, graphics improve reading comprehension, especially if students are reading for new information (Anderson, 1977).

Other Benefits of Chapter Survey. There is little doubt that survey procedures help students to discover important information in a textbook. Research by Drabin-Partenio and Maloney (1982) shows why we need to teach students to recognize the value of surveying. These authors discovered that the college freshmen with whom they worked had trouble placing what they read into a relative framework. We can infer from this that teaching students to recognize the author's schema will have a salutary effect. In any case, students who use the survey method are forced to identify content that is meant to be assimilated.

Active Study Methods

After completing the survey, the student will be ready to begin the process of reducing data to manageable levels for storage and retrieval. To lessen the time required for a particular lesson, note cards should be prepared. During the survey steps, the student will encounter material that it is obviously important to learn. It now becomes the student's job to predict or anticipate examination questions. This approach requires active rather than passive study methods, because only the former will result in heightened comprehension.

Comprehension of textbook material is simply a matter of making connections between new information and knowledge already stored in the brain. But, how can students activate their memories? Many authorities believe that it can best be accomplished through visual imagery—building picture associations for words, names, and so forth. To remember, one probably synthesizes a picture or schema. One remembers what is seen in visual memory. The trick is to connect new ideas with old through techniques of association. One of the more effective methods for making connections is mnemonics. Mnemonics are association "hooks" that help one recover information from memory.

Devising mnemonics requires the student to create associations that in turn improve mental processing. The more bizarre the mental image conjured up by the mnemonic, the more effective the recall of data from memory. The method, of course, is not new. The value of associative imagery was recognized by the Greeks and Romans, and in later years it was used by such scholars as Thomas Aquinas and Francis Bacon (Russell, 1979).

Textbook lists lend themselves to mnemonics, especially if the following strategies are employed: First, isolate key words and underline them. Second, highlight the first letter. Third, rearrange the letters to make a sense or nonsense word (acronym), or arrange them in alphabetical order. Fourth, print the mnemonic on a note card in red—for visual memory—and write what each letter stands for in lead pencil. Figure 2 shows how one can use mnemonics to master lists.

Because the preparation of study cards is an active process, students will find that study time is profitably spent. Challenging vocabulary, lists, enumerated points, diagrams, and theories are just some of the data that lend themselves to study cards and overlearning. This study design precludes loss of time to daydreaming, particularly for students who find it difficult to concentrate.

Overlearning

Aristotle formulated one of the earliest laws of learning with his dictum "To impress, express." The Romans expressed much the same idea in one of their cardinal rules for proper education, "Repetition is the mother of study." Few would deny that memory can be strengthened through repetition, but drill must be meaningful. Mouthing is parroting; minding makes the difference. Students will nonetheless find it helpful to recite aloud when attempting to overlearn material. Extensive studies show that one of the most effective means of preventing memory loss is to convey the information to someone as soon as possible after it has been acquired. Reciting aloud seems to aid in the storage of information. Scientists are not sure why this is so, but hearing one-self recite something helps to lock it into memory. Students often go to the trouble of organizing information and making note cards, but they fail to follow through by forcing themselves to recite. Reading the study cards silently is not enough. They must be read aloud.

Figure 2. How to Master Lists

EXAMPLE :

<u>Personnel and Management Criteria</u>

High Quality Employees
Personnel Relations
Company Size Relative to Competition
Record of Reaching Objectives
Top Management Amicability
Top Management Training and Depth
Profitability

STEP 1. Underline key words or phrases.

High <u>Quality</u> Employees
Personnel <u>Relations</u>
Company <u>Size</u> Relative to Competition
<u>Record</u> <u>of</u> <u>Reaching</u> Objectives
<u>Top</u> <u>Management</u> <u>Amicability</u>
<u>Top</u> <u>Management</u> <u>Training</u> and Depth
<u>Profitability</u>

STEP 2. Isolate first letter of each key word or phrase.

Q   R   S   R-of-R   T   T   P

STEP 3. Alphabetize the letters.

P   Q   R   R-of-R   S   T   T

STEP 4. Write mnemonic on note card with key letters highlighted for visual
memory.

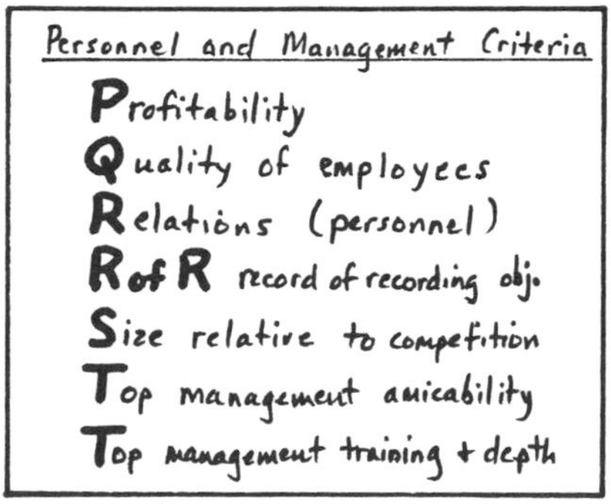

Personnel and Management Criteria

Profitability
Quality of employees
Relations (personnel)
R of **R** record of recording obj.
Size relative to competition
Top management amicability
Top management training + depth

Timing is also important. Note cards have to be reviewed quickly every twenty-four hours for seven successive days to assure storage in long-term memory. If a student learns several terms on Monday but fails to look at the terms again until Wednesday, the student may forget as much as 80 percent of the data.

The human brain seems to have an almost infinite capacity for memory. Some scientists have speculated that an average brain, which takes up only one tenth of a cubic foot of space, can store up to 199 billion different bits of information. The retrieval process is still a mystery, but this much is known: The brain is an electrochemical machine that requires proper fuel for efficient operation. A balanced diet, which includes protein, is essential for learning. The importance of protein intake on brain neurotransmitters has been reported by Restak (1979). Two important neurotransmitters are dependent on diet. Serotonin, formed from amino acids, and acetylcholine, the most common neurotransmitter in the human brain, both depend for their formation on diet. Normal human memory depends on acetylcholine, which is manufactured in the brain from choline. Choline is found in eggs, soybeans, liver, fish, and lecithin.

Conclusion

Since the early 1900s, most educational philosophers have agreed that one major role of education is to devise ways and means of improving the learning process. Today, faculty members across the nation recognize that students have difficulty learning assignments. Adult students returning to college find assignments laborious, time-consuming, and agonizing (Maxwell, 1979). One writer (Perry, 1979) advocated several years ago that students be provided with skills that help them to develop a flexible attack on different forms of study. He also suggested that instructors help students to put skills to work on long assignments.

"The ultimate aim of instruction is to prepare the student to successfully complete the typical assignments given in college courses" (Trillin, 1980, p. 127). The extensive, in-depth analysis of the Bullock Committee (Thackray, 1975) revealed that specific reading techniques can improve learning efficiency in the content fields. Committee members concluded that teachers should help students to acquire these skills. Instructors should know the demands of their own subject and the way in which students can best be helped to meet them. Few today would disagree with the view that the most critical element influencing the success or failure of educational programs is the quality of instruction (Miller, 1982). This view, however, seems to surprise some teachers of older students (Thackray, 1975).

Perhaps it is time for all content area teachers to concentrate on giving students the tools for rapid extraction of textbook information through recognition of an author's schema as reflected in the textbook and for memory techniques that enhance reduction and storage of knowledge for later retrieval. Mastery of these skills will result in improved comprehension and a more satisfying experience for students who must cope with college textbooks.

References

Anderson, R. C. "The Notion of Schemata and the Educational Enterprise." In R. C. Anderson, R. J. Spiro, and W. E. Montague (Eds.), *Schooling and the Acquisition of Knowledge.* Hillsdale, N.J.: Erlbaum, 1977.

Doctorow, M., Marks, C., and Wittrock, M. C. "Generative Processes in Reading Comprehension." *Journal of Educational Psychology,* 1978, *70* (2), 109–118.

Drabin-Partenio, I., and Maloney, W. H. "A Study of the Background Knowledge of Three Groups of College Freshmen." *Journal of Reading,* 1982, *25* (5), 430–434.

Mandler, J. M., and Johnson, M. S. "Remembrances of Things Parsed: Story, Structure, and Recall." *Cognitive Psychology,* 1977, 9 (6), 11–151.

Maxwell, M. *Improving Student Learning Skills: A Comprehensive Guide to Successful Practices and Programs for Increasing the Performance of Underprepared Students.* San Francisco: Jossey-Bass, 1979.

Meyer, B. J. F., and Freedle, R. *The Effects of Different Discourse Types on Recall.* Princeton, N.J.: Educational Testing Service, 1979.

Miller, B. S. "Bringing the Microcomputer into the Junior High: A Success Story From Florida." *Phi Delta Kappan,* 1982, *63* (5), 320.

Perry, W. G., Jr. "Students' Use and Misuse of Reading Skills: A Report to the Harvard Faculty." In M. Maxwell, *Improving Student Learning Skills: A Comprehensive Guide to Successful Practices and Programs for Increasing the Performance of Underprepared Students.* San Francisco: Jossey-Bass, 1979.

Restak, R. M. *The Brain: The Last Frontier.* New York: Doubleday, 1979.

Reading, Thinking, and Writing: Results From the 1979–80 National Assessment of Reading and Literature. Denver, Colo.: National Assessment of Educational Progress, 1981.

Russell, P. *The Brain Book.* New York: Hawthorn Books, 1979.

Thackray, D. (Ed.). *A Language for Life: Report of the Bullock Committee.* (ED 123 574).

Trillin, A. S. and associates. *Teaching Basic Skills in College: A Guide to Objectives, Skills Assessment, Course Content, Teaching Methods, Support Services, and Administration.* San Francisco: Jossey-Bass, 1980.

Ann S. Algier is coordinator of developmental education resources in the Office of Undergraduate Studies at Eastern Kentucky University (Richmond, Kentucky). She is an associate professor and former chairperson of the Department of Learning Skills. She is author of Everything You Need to Know About Learning *(Kendall/Hunt, 1979) and is currently vice-president of the Kentucky Council of the International Reading Association.*

*Listening comprehension has been demonstrated to be a significant
factor in attrition and retention among students in higher
education. What can professors do? More than fifty practical
suggestions are catalogued.*

Listening: Learning Tool and Retention Agent

Martha S. Conaway

Almost half of all entering freshmen will leave college before the beginning
of their sophomore year, and most will not return. Neither the students,
nor their families, nor colleges and universities can afford the resulting loss
of time, money, and reputation. Because of a universal concern, educational
and federal institutions have conducted research to identify the dissimilarities
of persisters and nonpersisters, to identify the causes of attrition, and to
design effective retention programs.

An abundance of information is available from studies conducted in
the separate areas of listening comprehension and attrition and retention in
postsecondary institutions. Despite all this information, a computer-assisted
search of the literature revealed that the variable of listening comprehension
had not been included as a possible factor in the attrition and retention of
college students. Recent research by the author has demonstrated that
listening comprehension is a highly significant factor in the academic
achievement and retention of college students.

Survey of Existing Literature

Attrition and Retention of Higher Education. The literature on attrition in
higher education contained four major types of research: census (in which

A. S. Algier, K. W. Algier (Eds.). *New Directions for College Learning Assistance:
Reading and Study Skills,* no. 8. San Francisco: Jossey-Bass, June 1982

counts were made and statistics were derived), autopsy (involving question-naires or ex post facto searches of school records) case study, and prediction (in which forecasts were based on past statistics). Very few longitudinal studies were done, and there was little attention to dropouts who eventually completed a degree. Statistics varied widely, with attrition being reported at rates ranging between 12 percent and 82 percent, while the mode ranged between 45 percent and 60 percent. Approximately 40 percent of entering freshmen finished school in four years (Fetters, 1977; Iffert, 1957; Pantages and Creedon, 1978; Ramist, 1981). About half of the freshmen had dropped out by the end of their first year; most left within the first six weeks of school. The probability of dropping out decreased as the number of semesters attended increased (Conaway, 1981). Other factors that were considered significant are a GPA less than 2.0 (Astin, 1975; Pantages and Creedon, 1978; Pedrini and Pedrini, 1977, 1978; Tinto, 1975), parents lacking in education (Tinto, 1975), married females (Lewis, 1979), and low-ability students in nonselective colleges (Astin, 1975; Demitroff, 1974; Summerskill, 1962).

Listening Comprehension. The literature on listening comprehension revealed that very few empirical studies had been conducted and that the studies that have been done are relatively recent. Researchers found that college students were expected to listen about 90 percent of class time (Taylor, 1973); that there was a significant positive relationship between listening comprehension and GPA (Amerson, 1974; Irvin, 1952; Montgomery, 1970; Nichols, 1948; Seymour, 1965); that a specific, discrete, objectively testable listening factor could be isolated and classified into subskills (Clark, 1973; Lundsteen, 1964; Spearritt, 1962); and that listening comprehension skills could be taught using sequential steps (Lundsteen and Wilson, 1979; Nichols, 1959). Researchers debated whether listening and reading influence each other or whether both are part of a single basic thinking skill (Devine, 1976; Lundsteen, 1979; Seymour, 1965; Spache, 1950).

Description of the Study

Beginning in 1978, data were gathered for a study conducted at Eastern Kentucky University, Richmond (EKU). This study investigated the contribution of listening comprehension to academic success or failure and to persistence or nonpersistence of college students, in itself and in interaction with seventy other variables.

The sample consisted of 418 Eastern Kentucky University students of both sexes and all class and achievement levels, between the ages of sixteen and fifty-seven. Subjects were obtained through voluntary enrollment in a college study skills course under normal registration procedures. The Brown-Carlsen Listening Comprehension Test (Brown-Carlsen) and the Nelson-Denny Reading Test (Nelson-Denny) were routinely given to all sections as part of the course. The subjects were divided into several subgroups: students with GPAs over or under 2.0, students eligible for academic dismissal, honor students, persisters, nonpersisters, and students who temporarily dropped out and returned, to name only a few. Correlations and tests were done on each variable, and the results on all variables were compared to determine whether the results remained unchanged.

From the date of the Brown-Carlsen testing, students were followed to record semesters completed or dropped and cumulative GPA. If a semester was not completed and the last recorded GPA was below the university's academic dismissal criterion for the student's class level, the student was judged to have failed and dropped out. Dropouts' transcript records were checked to determine whether an official transcript had been requested for another institution. If one had not, dropout status was confirmed, since a transcript is usually required when a student transfers to another school. Students who had returned after an absence of one or more semesters were designated as stopouts. All 418 subjects will be followed for ten years.

Results

From among seventy variables, gender, age, residence, class level, Nelson-Denny scores, American College Test (ACT) scores, and Brown-Carlsen scores were selected through multilinear regression analysis as most influential. The last three were highly significant, exhibiting a .0001 level of confidence when correlated with the academic attrition or retention of the total population. When students with GPAs below the minimum criterion were considered separately, listening comprehension achieved a much higher correlation to attrition or retention than did reading or ACT scores, as the following:

Spearman correlation coefficients show:
Brown-Carlsen -0.14320; $p < 0.2172$ on 76 observations.
ACT -0.00305; $p < 0.9809$ on 64 observations.
Nelson-Denny -0.00235; $p < 0.9839$ on 76 observations.

A chi-square test of independence was used to determine the relationship between listening comprehension ability and academic achievement as measured by GPAs. Students were divided into three subgroups: students at the academic dismissal level, honor students, and students between these two groups. Listening scores were grouped according to Brown-Carlsen levels: very low, low, average, high, and very high. Table 1 shows that five of the academic dismissal level students (4.42 percent) attained above-average listening comprehension scores, as compared to thirty-three (68.5 percent) of the honor students. No dismissal student earned a very high

Table 1. Brown-Carlsen Chi-Square Table

LEVEL FREQUENCY EXPECTED PERCENT ROW PCT COL PCT	BROWN-CARLSEN ACHIEVEMENT LEVELS				
	Very Low 1	Low 2	Average 3	High and Very High 4	TOTAL
1 DISMISSAL STUDENTS	27 10.00 6.46 35.53 49.09	17 14.00 4.07 22.37 22.08	27 28.70 6.46 35.53 17.09	5 23.30 1.20 6.58 3.91	76 18.18
2 AVERAGE STUDENTS	26 38.70 6.22 8.84 47.27	57 54.20 13.64 19.39 74.03	121 111.10 28.95 41.16 76.58	90 90.00 21.53 30.61 70.31	294 70.33
3 HONOR STUDENTS	2 6.30 0.48 4.17 3.64	3 8.80 0.72 6.25 3.90	10 18.10 2.39 20.83 6.33	33 14.70 7.89 68.75 25.78	48 11.48
TOTAL	55 13.16	77 18.42	158 37.80	128 30.62	418 100.00

STATISTICS FOR 2-WAY TABLES

CHI-SQUARE	82.430	DF= 6	PROB=0.0001
PHI	0.444		
CONTINGENCY COEFFICIENT	0.405		
CRAMER'S V	0.314		
LIKELIHOOD RATIO CHISQUARE	77.594	DF= 6	PROB=0.0001

Brown-Carlsen score, as compared to more than 10 percent of the honor students. Only two honor students (4.17 percent) earned very low scores, but almost half of the dismissal students (more than 49 percent) did. Seventy-one percent of the dismissal students earned below-average listening scores. Even when cells containing f < 5 were collapsed with neighboring cells and the test was rerun, the chi-square test demonstrated that a positive dependent relationship, highly significant at the .0001 level, existed between college student GPAs and listening comprehension.

For the total population, a negative correlation significant at the .001 level occurred between Brown-Carlsen raw scores and age at the testing date. Among deficiency students (GPA < 2.0), age and listening comprehension were negatively and significantly correlated at the .05 level. A correlation between age and listening comprehension was also found in the research of Belson (1952), Landry (1969), Logan (1960), and Rossiter (1970). Half of the dropouts had GPAs of less than 2.0. Among those eligible for dismissal, GPA and dropping out were negatively correlated and highly significant (p < .0003). Among first-semester dropouts, 57 percent had GPAs below the minimum criterion; the Brown-Carlsen subtests Recognizing Word Meanings was significant at .02, and Lecture Comprehension subtest was significant at .04 when correlated with GPA.

Discussion

Listening comprehension plays a more important part in the educational process, in academic achievement, and in student retention than educators have acknowledged. The very high first-semester attrition rate together with the extremely low listening comprehension scores of some entering freshmen emphasize the urgency of early identification of students with this skill deficiency. The use of a listening comprehension test in the standard admissions procedure would serve as a screening device, as an early alert to both advisor and student of potential problems, and as an indication of which entering freshmen should be encouraged to enroll in listening skills classes.

Past research concluded that listening comprehension can be taught, that listening skills acquisition is highly correlated with higher GPAs, and that higher GPAs are correlated with greater retention. The research conducted at EKU shows that listening comprehension is positively and significantly correlated with both GPA and retention. Therefore, the addition of listening skills courses to the curriculum would be a service both to students and to institutions. Since 57 percent of the first-semester dropouts had a GPA below the minimum criterion, it is imperative that listening skills courses be offered at the beginning of the fall semester and during the summer as college warm-up and Upward-Bound programs.

56

Listening is the first communication skill to be acquired in the natural sequence of human development (Jolly, 1980). It can be an effective method for teaching concepts in other communication skills (Cleveland, 1980), first by identifying examples through listening, then by finding them in reading and by producing them in spoken and written forms. Main idea, supporting detail, and cause and effect are just a few of the concepts that can be generalized from one communication mode to another.

Because age at the time the test was taken was negatively and significantly correlated at .001 level for the total population and at .05 for students with a GPA < 2.0, it is highly probable that students beyond the normal college age of eighteen to twenty-two and that students who have been away from the classroom for more than two years will be less efficient listeners. Research studies have confirmed this for persons outside academe. This seems to indicate that a listening comprehension test can be an excellent diagnostic device if an older student is earning poor grades.

It is absolutely essential for "ear training" (Redden, 1981) to begin at birth and to be maintained throughout life. Artists talk about visual literacy, and persons can be taught to become more visually aware of the total environment. It is equally, if not more, important to be aurally literate from infancy, because listening is both the first step to language acquisition and the foundation of all other communication skills. Life involves listening, more than any other skill. Poor listening ability diminishes full life to the degree of one's listening deficiency.

Conclusions

Analyzing the data gathered on 418 students, EKU researchers drew eight conclusions: Listening comprehension as measured by the Brown-Carlsen was an extremely important factor (p < .0001) in attrition and retention; the mean Brown-Carlsen percentile score for persisting students was 20 percentiles higher than the score of first-semester dropouts. Listening comprehension as measured by the Brown-Carlsen was an extremely important factor (p < .0001) in cumulative GPAs. Listening comprehension as measured by the Brown-Carlsen became an increasingly significant problem as student age at the time of the test increased, especially among students carrying a cumulative GPA of less than 2.0; subtests by descending order of significance were Following Directions, Immediate Recall, Lecture Comprehension, and Recognizing Transitions. First-semester attrition rates can be drastically reduced by giving potential underachievers classes in listening skills that stress lecture comprehension and use of context clues. Among students guaranteed dismissal because of unsatisfactory GPAs, the Brown-Carlsen correlation was 77 percent higher than either the Nelson-Denny or the ACT; for this reason, the Brown-Carlsen should be given to all incoming students presenting low previous GPAs or ACT composite scores of 12 or below. More than 70 percent of students with serious academic problems do not adequately comprehend and efficiently process what they hear. Among the students who fail, deficient listening skills were a stronger factor than reading skills or academic aptitude as measured by Nelson-Denny and ACT scores, respectively. Finally, listening skills courses should be added to the general curriculum and made available to all entering freshmen during their first semester on campus.

Implications for Educators

The more deeply that professors become immersed in their content area, the more they seem to focus on the quantity and the subject matter of their courses, and the less they seem to focus on teaching techniques and instructor behaviors that enhance or inhibit student comprehension of that subject matter. There are many options open to professors who wish to assist students in receiving, processing, and understanding aural information. The amount of assistance that individual students need will vary with their characteristic mode of learning, their hearing acuity, and their accumulated background knowledge, to name only some factors.

This chapter will conclude with an inventory of ways in which professors can help students to listen more efficiently and to understand and remember more of what they hear in the classroom. The inventory has been organized into ten general categories. Some suggestions are already part of good, everyday classroom management. Others may be buried in the college methods class notes of many experienced teachers. Some suggestions will be new, but all will be helpful.

Eliminate Class Distractions

- Acknowledge and deal quickly with major class disruptions.
- Minimize professor-originated distractions, such as those caused by personal mannerisms, clanking jewelry, provocative fashions, and obscene or profane talk.
- Minimize content-originated distractions that can arise from inflammatory words and terms. Inflammatory topics sometimes attract rather than distract.
- Minimize, label, and otherwise de-emphasize lecture digressions.
- Turn off audiovisual equipment as soon as possible after use. Light, motor noise, and used slides or transparencies detract from presentation of subsequent material.
- When objects and realia are incorporated in the presentation, keep them out of sight both before and after they are used.

Consider the Physical Environment

- Check the wall behind the speaker's podium. Are there any distractions, such as a clock to watch, a window or light that tends to make listeners drowsy or that causes the speaker to be in shadow or silhouette?
- Check the size of the room. Can audiovisuals be seen and heard by everyone without distortion?
- In discussions, can everyone hear and see everyone else? In question-and-answer sessions, it is a good practice for the leader to repeat questions posed by members of the audience before an answer is given.
- Check student seating arrangements. Are distractors seated on the periphery and poor listeners and those easily distracted seated closer to the speaker?

Observe the Students

- Read the body language of class members. Students who are poor listeners and slow writers often send nonverbal signals to the teacher when something needs explanation or deceleration.
- Note students' tension level. Relieve inordinate tension with a change of pace, an anecdote, an alternate activity.
- Pay special attention to older students. If they begin to have difficulty in class, they may need listening training.

Be Aware of Time

- Allow students time for processing aural information, so that it can be stored in long-term memory. Use examples, questions concerning the topic, or discussion.
- Allow time for note-taking on important points by giving supporting details and examples before continuing on to the next point.
- Allow time for a question-and-answer session following a presentation, so that orally presented information can be clarified and notes can be corrected.
- Be aware of the time differential between the speed of speech and the speed of thought. Much woolgathering can take place in the interim.
- Lengthy sessions without breaks or change of style and pace are not conducive to good listening comprehension.

Lecture Effectively

- Be organized. The brain responds well to organized information and remembers it longer. Lecturing from an outline can be as helpful to the listeners as it can to the speaker.

- Share the outline with the class. Display it on an overhead transparency, and expose its points one at a time. Distribute it as a handout. Write it on the chalkboard.
- Identify, define, and spell new terms, jargon, or unusual vocabulary. Some educators feel that this is best done before the lecture. Others prefer to do so as each term is used.
- If a lecture must be read in its entirety, read with expression, vary the speed of delivery, and try to maintain eye contact with the students.
- Avoid both monotonous and affected delivery.
- Face the class when speaking. A surprising number of students have some hearing loss and unconsciously read lips and facial expressions. Teachers who frequently write on chalkboards or who use audiovisual and laboratory equipment often make this mistake.
- Refocus class attention occasionally by changing position at the podium, lecturing from another spot in the room, introducing appropriate objects and graphics, or using provocative questions and statements.
- Avoid passing items around the class during the lecture. Students cannot examine the article, listen, and take notes simultaneously.
- If papers are to be passed out or pages turned, wait until the rustling has ceased and full attention is gained before attempting to speak.
- Vary the lecture situation occasionally by inviting guest speakers, assigning student reports, or holding panel discussions.

Emphasize Main Points

- Find some nonverbal means of signaling main points, and use it consistently.
- Write main points on the chalkboard, or use an overhead projector to display them.
- Repeat important statements.
- Use transitional words and phrases to make it easy for students to determine the relationship of points in the lecture and to take accurate notes.
- Conclude all lectures with summary statements that concisely reiterate salient points.

Maintain Student Attention

- Smile! A good-natured speaker attracts audience attention.
- Be positive! Speak enthusiastically about the subject matter to be considered. Enthusiasm is contagious.
- Vary facial expressions, using them to underscore what is being spoken about.

- Vary voice tone, pace, and style of speaking, using these features to emphasize main points and to refocus listener attention.
- Give instructions once—at the most, twice. Students fall into a habit of withholding attention until they are ready to execute instructions and then ask for an instant replay.
- Use attention-getters appropriate to the lesson. Keep them concealed before and after use. Heightened curiosity, surprise, even verbal fanfare all operate to hold student attention and motivate listening comprehension.
- Help students to collect their thoughts by reviewing relevant previously taught material, by creating a verbal context or setting for new material, or by explaining the need for or possible applications of the lesson content to be presented.

Employ All the Senses

- Vary student tasks within the class period to rest ears and allow time for information to pass from short-term to long-term memory. Intersperse listening with activities requiring students to use other skills and senses: asking questions, discussion, reading and reacting to short passages, writing responses to lecture points, viewing demonstrations or audiovisuals, role-playing that reinforces a point made in the oral presentation.
- Capitalize on the synergism available from multiple storage areas. Each organ of perception uses different areas of the brain. Information can be stored visually, aurally, and otherwise, so that information stored in one area of the brain can be cross-referenced with information stored in another, One sense can reinforce the recall ability of another. The more student senses that a professor can engage in a presentation, the more ways that students have to store information and the greater the chances of recall (Higbee, 1977; Paivio and Csapo, 1973).
- Use a picture. Long before the days of empirical research, the Chinese were telling us that one picture is worth a thousand words. Sources are myriad, and the means for use are many. The effectiveness of stick figures and crude chalk drawings should not be underrated, nor should the value of mental imagery be overlooked.
- Use the real thing. Nothing engages the senses as well as realia, which can be seen, handled, manipulated, listened to, tasted, and smelled. Nothing preserves a verbal presentation better than realia.

Guide the Listener

- Point out why students need the content being presented or what they will gain personally from applying it.

- Refer to a syllabus, placing the current lesson in its context by pointing to its position in the sequential unfolding of the broad topic.
- Introduce a lecture by creating a verbal setting that can be pictured mentally by students. Imagining will aid understanding now and recall later.
- If the presentation is to include audiovisual material, provide a handout that enables students to anticipate major points and to make notes as the presentation proceeds.
- If the presentation is to be a lecture, begin by announcing the lesson objectives.
- Begin with the known or where the student is now, and then build a bridge to the unknown with a brief review of the previous lesson, an example from everyday life, or an experience common to everyone. It is easier to listen to and remember information on topics about which one has some prior basic knowledge.
- Include frequent internal summaries in a presentation, to help students to keep the overall organization in mind. Some speakers do this as each new major point is added.

Additional Suggestions

- Cite other sources, readings, texts to which students can refer for further study or investigation.
- Use every opportunity to pass on instruction in concentration techniques, vocabulary expansion, mnemonics, and ear training.
- Warn students of the permanent hearing loss incurred when delicate hair follicles inside the ear are destroyed by loud music and harsh noises.
- Ask someone to videotape a personal class presentation. Analyze professor strengths, weaknesses, individual student and teacher behaviors, and teacher-student and student-student interaction. Much can be learned when we can see ourselves as others see us and hear ourselves as others hear us.

References

Amerson, E. M. "The Effect of Instruction in Listening on the Development of Listening Comprehension Skills of Disadvantaged Postsecondary Youth." Unpublished doctoral dissertation, University of Kentucky, 1974.

Astin, A. W. *Preventing Students from Dropping Out.* San Francisco: Jossey-Bass, 1975.

Belson, W. A. "Topic for Tonight: A Study of Comprehensibility." *B.B.C. Quarterly,* 1952, *7,* 94–99.

Clark, M. L. *Hierarchical Structures on Comprehension Skills.* Vol. 2. Hawthorn, Victoria: Australian Council for Educational Research, 1973.

Cleveland, B. "Active Listening Yields Better Discussion." *Social Studies,* 1980, *71* (5), 218–221.

Conaway, M. S. "Listening Comprehension as a Factor in Attrition/Retention in Higher Education." Unpublished doctoral dissertation, Southern Illinois University at Carbondale, 1981.

Demitroff, J. F. "Student Persistence." *College and University,* 1974, *49,* 553–567.

Devine, T. G. "Listening and Reading." Paper presented at the annual meeting of the Reading Association of Ireland, Dublin, 1976.

Fetters, W. B. *Withdrawal from Institutions of Higher Education: An Appraisal with Longitudinal Data Involving Diverse Institutions,* Washington, D.C.: U.S. Office of Education, 1977.

Higbee, K. L. *Your Memory: How It Works and How to Improve It.* Englewood Cliffs, N.J.: Prentice-Hall, 1977.

Iffert, R. E. *Retention and Withdrawal of College Students.* Washington, D.C.: U.S. Department of Health, Education, and Welfare, 1957.

Irvin, C. E. "An Analysis of Certain Aspects of a Listening Training Program Among College Freshmen at Michigan State College." Unpublished doctoral dissertation, Michigan State College, 1952.

Jolly, T. "ERIC/RCS Report: Listen My Children and You Shall Read." *Language Arts,* 1980, *57* (2), 214–218.

Landry, D. L. "The Neglect of Listening." *Elementary English,* 1969, *46,* 599–605.

Lewis, C. J. *Eastern Kentucky University: An Institutional Study on Student Retention.* Richmond: Retention Study Steering Committee, Eastern Kentucky University, 1979.

Logan, L. M. *Teaching the Young Child.* Boston: Houghton Mifflin, 1960.

Lundsteen, S. W. "Teaching and Testing Critical Listening in the Fifth and Sixth Grades." *Elementary English,* 1964, *41,* 743–747, 752.

Lundsteen, S. W. *Listening: Its Impact at All Levels on Reading and the Other Language Arts.* (Rev. ed.) Urbana, Ill.: National Council of Teachers of English, 1979.

Lundsteen, S. W. and Wilson, J. A. R. "Permanency of Gains for Children's Problem-Solving Processes and Subabilities." *Educational Research Quarterly,* 1979, *4* (1), 41–49.

Montgomery, M. A. "An Investigation of Students Who Succeed Academically and Those Who Do Not Succeed Academically in a Community College." Unpublished doctoral dissertation, University of Pittsburgh, 1970.

Nichols, R. G. "Factors Accounting for Difference in Comprehension of Materials Presented Orally in the Classroom." Unpublished doctoral dissertation, State University of Iowa, 1948.

Nichols, R. G. "Listening." In *American Educator Encyclopedia,* Vol. 6. Lake Bluff, Il.: United Educators Incorporated, 1959.

Paivio, A., and Csapo, K. "Picture Superiority in Free Recall: Imagery or Dual Coding." *Cognitive Psychology,* 1973, *5,* 176–206.

Pantages, T. J. and Creedon, C. F. "Studies in College Attrition: 1950–1975." *Review of Educational Research,* 1978, *48* (1), 49–101.

Pedrini, B. C. and Pedrini, D. T. "Multivariate Prediction of Attrition/Persistence for Disadvantaged and Control Collegians." *College Student Journal,* 1977, *11,* 239–242.

Pedrini, B. C., and Pedrini, D. T. "Evaluating Experimental and Control Programs for Attrition/Persistence." *Journal of Educational Research,* 1978, *71* (4), 234–237.

Ramist, L. *College Student Attrition and Retention.* New York: College Entrance Examination Board, 1981.

Redden, J. E. "On Expanding the Meaning of Applied Linguistics: A Suggestion for Training Linguists and Language Teachers in Field Linguistics." *The Linguistic Reporter,* 1981, *23* (5), 3–5.

Rossiter, C. M., Jr. "Chronological Age and Listening of Adult Students." *Adult Education Journal,* 1970, *21* (1), 40–43.

Seymour, P. J. "A Study of the Relationship Between the Communications Skills and a Selected Set of Predictors and of the Relationship Among the Communication Skills." Unpublished doctoral dissertation, University of Minnesota, 1965.

Spache, G. D. "Construction and Validation of a Work-Type Auditory Comprehension Reading Test." *Educational and Psychological Measurement,* 1950, *10,* 249–253.

Spearritt, D. L. *Listening Comprehension: A Factorial Analysis.* Melbourne: Australian Council for Educational Research, 1962.

Summerskill, J. "Dropouts from College." In R. N. Sanford (Ed.), *The American College: A Psychological and Social Interpretation of the Higher Learning.* New York: Wiley, 1962.

Taylor, S. E. *Listening* What Research Says to the Teacher. No. 29. Washington, D.C.: National Education Association, 1964 (ED 026 120).

Tinto, V. "Dropouts from Higher Education: A Theoretical Synthesis of Recent Research." *Review of Educational Research,* 1975, *45* (1), 89–125.

Martha S. Conaway has taught reading, study skills, and English as a second language in the Department of Learning Skills at Eastern Kentucky University since 1976. Prior to joining the university, she was involved with adult education, staff training, and curriculum design for the Kentucky Department for Human Resources. She is coauthor of Resourcery *and is vice-president of the Kentucky chapter of Teachers of English to Speakers of Other Languages (TESOL).*

Success on the essay examination requires more than knowledge of course content and a clear writing style.

Analyze, Synthesize, Organize: An Active Approach to Essay Exam Preparation

David R. Hubin
Susan J. Lesyk

Educators frequently criticize their students' emphasis on test performance. Certainly, when this concern degenerates into the question "Do we have to know this for the test?" something of the joy of learning has been lost. However, in the academic setting, where learning and even aptitude for learning are demonstrated by performance on examinations, it should be no surprise that students are often confused about the role of testing in the learning process. Rather than lamenting students' emphasis on tests, we as educators need to demonstrate to students how an early and consistent concern with tests—a concern that develops the skills of analysis, synthesis, and reasoning—forms an excellent underpinning of effective learning.

Course Analysis as Test Preparation

When learning specialists ask students how they plan to study for an examination, the typical response is this: "Tonight, I'm going to look over

A. S. Algier, K. W. Algier (Eds.). *New Directions for College Learning Assistance: Reading and Study Skills,* no. 8. San Francisco: Jossey-Bass, June 1982

my notes; tomorrow, I'm going to go over the textbook; the next day, I'll review the outside reading." Despite their overriding concern with test performance, students commonly pursue an approach to studying that overlooks concrete tasks, as implied by the expressions *look over* and *go over* and that fails to reflect the integrated themes present in a course. If students are to enhance both their learning and their performance on examinations, this approach to study must change early in the term.

All too often, students approach their courses passively, without academic expectations. In contrast, active learners approach a course with major questions already in mind, the answers to which provide a basis for selective reading, a framework for note-taking, and clues to appropriate test questions. These questions include: What are the professor's assumptions, biases, teaching objectives? What relationships among the topics are emphasized? What are the unifying themes?

Seeking answers to questions such as these is the first step in examination preparation; it begins the process of course analysis, and it lays the foundation for effective study. Even the academically aggressive student often overlooks the wealth of information that is often contained in a professor's course description. Consider, for example, the following description of an introductory history course:

> *Course Description:* U.S. History, 1865–Present
>
> This course will introduce students to an interpretation of America, a complex society shaped by institutions and ideologies. Students will study the way in which the material conditions of peoples' lives influence the way they think and, in turn, how they make political decisions. Attention will be given to the way in which institutions respond to and are shaped by the problems of social reform which have come about through modernization. Lectures and reading will stress the institutions through which people sustain their society and the ideologies by which they rationalize their actions.

In this course description, the professor highlights topics, reveals emphases, and suggests themes; moreover, he discloses a priori assumptions about the subject matter; for example, that material conditions shape people's ideas and that these ideas, in turn, influence the shape of institutions.

One approach to improving students' abilities to gain useful information from course descriptions is to have them paraphrase the material (Bazerman, 1982). If students paraphrase carefully, then turn each statement into a question or learning task, they will have a basis both for integrating the material and for generating the questions to be answered in their course of study. Returning to the course description just cited, we can predict that students who analyze the second and third sentences correctly will decide that one question that they may be called upon to answer at the end of the course is this: "Use examples from lecture and reading to describe and illustrate the ways in which problems created by modernization have led to changes in institutions and ideas." Students should modify and refine their questions throughout the course as they gain information from readings, lectures, and discussions. Major thematic questions provide academic purposes for reading assignments and lectures. Rather than asking why they have to read the material at all, students who pursue this questioning ask how the material reflects or illustrates a particular theme.

The task of synthesizing course material from discrete lectures and then of integrating lectures with readings can be accomplished only after this initial step of analysis is completed. In other words, one must dissect, examine, and weigh the importance of the parts before one can make sense of the whole.

Content Synthesis as Test Preparation

It is usually only a week or two before an examination that students begin to translate their studying for a particular course into preparing for the test. If pretest study follows a term of active analysis, then students will be in a good position to synthesize and integrate course material. Rereading and reanalysis of the course description and syllabus should precede a rapid overview of the notes and chapter headings from the course. Wood (1978, p. 183) refers to this process as one of developing a "personal table of contents for the course." These activities provide a perspective on the scope of the course that enables students to make decisions on how to focus their study and manage their time.

One method of integrating course material involves use of summary sheets. Each major topic drawn from the rapid overview becomes the heading on a blank sheet of paper. As students research these topics, they associate the relevant factual material with the appropriate headings. Students in the U.S. history course noted here might have summary sheets headed *industrialization, labor organizations, the Progressive Movement, the New Deal, urbanization,* and so forth. These topics become the key words in self-generated study questions. Instead of passively looking over their notes, students actively examine relationships and seek answers.

In the process of overviewing the course and developing summary sheets, students should look for natural relationships among topics that can help them to predict examination questions. If there are two themes, theses, or institutions with notable similarities, the professor is likely to ask a compare-and-contrast question. In the U.S. history course, for example, students who notice that the Progressives have significant points of comparison with the New Deal reformers or that the effects of the two world wars on labor warrant comparison will recognize the potential for a compare-and-contrast relationship.

Although students who can accurately predict test questions are sometimes held in awe by peers, they have done nothing more than critically analyze, formally or intuitively, the clues provided in the course structure and in the course content.

Logical Steps in Prewriting

The intellectual activities of analyzing and synthesizing course material can enable students to predict the general exam content with a fair amount of reliability. In the examination situation itself, however, there is a danger that students who feel comfortable with their knowledge of a topic may unconsciously modify a question or even ignore parts of it in order to demonstrate the factual knowledge that they have gained. To avoid this, the mental activities of analysis and synthesis must be extended to the prewriting process in the examination itself.

When staff of the University of Oregon's learning center asked faculty members to voice their concerns regarding the answers that students wrote in response to essay questions, professors complained that students did not answer questions directly and succinctly, that students did not organize their answers effectively, and that students did not balance generalizations with specifics or associate detail with unifying themes. When these concerns were shared with students who attended workshops on writing effective essay exams, the students were surprised that professors seemed more concerned with problems of structure and logic than with problems of content. Students acknowledged that professors encouraged them to outline their answers before beginning to write. However, most students were not convinced that preplanning was more than a waste of time. "Under time pressure and without the luxury of a rough draft, I have to focus on what I'm saying, not on how I'm saying it," commented one student. "I quickly try to outline my answer before I begin to write, but I never know if my outline is any better organized than my answer would be without it." Indeed, if the time invested results merely in a linear outline that reminds its writer of points to be covered in the intended answer, then students' skepticism seems justified. However, if the prewriting activity were to result instead in such a complete picture of the answer that students could visualize the content of the introduction, the structure of and the relationship among the paragraphs, and even the key words for topic sentences, then their doubts would dissipate.

Because the approach to organizing an essay answer varies with the type of essay question asked, students need to develop the logical skill of determining what relationship exists among the variables in the question and why. A trace question, for example, implies a relationship that is quite different from that raised by a compare-and-contrast question or by an evaluate question. Just as different types of question imply different relationships, they also require students to engage in different patterns of reasoning that lead to different patterns of organization. Determining the relationship among variables requires a certain sophistication when the imperative verb in the question is not easy to translate into a concrete task. Professors often ask students to *discuss, comment,* or *explain.* Unfortunately, for many students, such requests are no more organizationally directive than a request to tell all that they know about the topic.

The first step in the prewriting process, then, is to ascertain the relationship implicit in the question, even if the imperative verb is non-directive, then to identify a concrete task that will appropriately explore the relationship. Suppose that the professor of the U.S. history course that we have been using as an example distributed an essay test that included this question: "The Progressive Movement was a direct response to the problems of industrialization. Discuss." Instead of launching into a discussion of the Progressive Movement and the problems of industrialization, the canny student would first determine the relationship between the Progressive Movement and the problems of industrialization. That is, the student would paraphrase the question in order to reveal an explicit cause-effect relationship. Thus, the student might restructure the question like this: "What were the problems of industrialization that caused a response which we label the Progressive Movement?"

In the next step of the prewriting process, the student constructs a conceptual chart or matrix that indicates the relationship between the variables and that serves to separate general issues of consideration from supporting detail and examples. Figure 1 charts the essay question that we have used as an example.

Brainstorming the content of the answer, then, is reserved until the student has a conceptual structure in which to categorize the material in terms of both content and level of specificity (Figure 2).

Figure 1. The Initial Pre-Writing Matrix

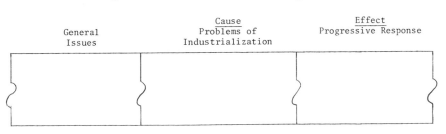

	Cause	Effect
General Issues	Problems of Industrialization	Progressive Response

Figure 2. The Completed Pre-Writing Matrix

General Issues	Cause Problems of Industrialization	Effect Progressive Response
Social	Urbanization Change in family New labor conditions New social conditions	Muckraking -- Spargo Settlement houses Working condition laws Brandeis Brief
Political	Growth of bossism Tweed	Muckraking -- Baker LaFollette Reforms Party platform -- 1912
Economic	Trusts Standard Oil Wealth distribution	Muckraking -- Tarbell Anti-trust legislation railroad regulation

By evaluating the content of the completed matrix, the student can quickly construct an introduction that defines the nature of the relationship and the scope of the essay, previews the major issues of consideration, and, if appropriate, offers a thesis statement. The student is in a position to begin the essay with confidence, by directly addressing the question asked: "The Progressive Movement was a direct response to the social, political, and economic problems caused by the process of industrialization in the post-Civil War decades of the nineteenth century." This introductory sentence responds directly to the question by indicating a causal relationship between the problems of industrialization and the Progressive Movement. Moreover, it previews the topics to be addressed and the order in which they will be presented.

In order to complete the matrix, students must distinguish between concrete facts, examples, and illustrations and the abstract concepts, themes, and general issues that the specifics support. Thus, once completed, the matrix provides the student with a verbal icon of the essay as a whole. By glancing down the column under "General Issues," students can visualize how many paragraphs (or major sections) their essay will contain. Topic sentences are easily formed by relating the general issue to the task of the essay. For example, the topic sentence of the first paragraph in the body of the essay might be: "Industrialization created social problems and dislocations that prompted demands for social reform." Similarly, the topic sentence of the second paragraph would relate the political problems of industrialization to pressure for reform.

By glancing across each row, students can visualize the internal content and deductive structure of individual paragraphs. When following the matrix, students are obligated to "downshift" (Christensen, 1967, p. 56), an effective technique for developing a paragraph structure that moves from the general to the specific. For example, the topic sentence for the paragraph on social issues would be supported by the specific social problems noted under the column "Problems of Industrialization"—urbanization, new labor conditions, and so forth. The specific social problems must, in turn, be related to the specific responses noted under the column "Progressive Response"—settlement houses and labor legislation. Each paragraph develops in this manner, following general statements based on key words in the primary, general issues column with specific statements of support based on key words in the secondary columns.

It is not enough to tell students to outline their thoughts before beginning an essay. Instead, we must teach the logical skills necessary for productive prewriting; that is, prewriting that results in student essays that have strong introductions, that are effectively organized by unifying themes, and that balance generalizations with support.

Conclusion

Students are frustrated when they find that knowledge of course content and a clear writing style are not sufficient for effective performance on the essay exam. For many, essay examinations become a mysterious ritual in which their future grade is cast to highly subjective, if not arbitrary, fates. However, if students are helped to view exam preparation not as a disjointed addendum to academic work but as a culmination of active learning—a culmination based on critical analysis, synthesis, and organized thought—this frustration can be resolved.

References

Bazerman, C. *The Informed Writer.* Boston: Houghton Mifflin, 1982.
Christensen, F. *Notes Toward a New Rhetoric.* New York: Harper & Row, 1967.
Wood, N. V. *College Reading and Study Skills.* New York: Holt, Rinehart and Winston, 1978.

David R. Hubin is director of the Learning Resources Center at the University of Oregon. Previously, he taught in learning centers at the University of Texas and the University of California, Irvine.

Susan J. Lesyk is assistant director of the Learning Resources Center at the University of Oregon and coordinator of its Writing Lab. At the University of Oregon, she has developed and offered day-long workshops on the essay exam.

*Because of the unique characteristics of adult students, including
their motivation for attendance, their intense desire to succeed,
and the competition of their other roles with their role as student,
adult students greatly need assistance in the development of
essential skills.*

Factors That Influence Academic Achievement in the over Twenty-Five Age Group

Suzanne Teegarden
Robert E. Tarvin

The closing years of the twentieth century will place special demands on
institutions of higher education to develop and support more learning assistance programs. Those involved in learning assistance programs will be
required to recognize the special needs of the new clienteles that will attend
our postsecondary institutions. The Carnegie Council on Policy Studies in
Higher Education (1980, p. 53) projects that "one half of the students in the
classrooms of 2000 would not have been there if the composition of 1960 had
been continued." The new clientele that composes this new half will include
persons twenty-five years old and older, white females, blacks, Hispanics,
part-time students, high school students, and foreign students, and retention
will be increased.

Each of these special groups of new students will require learning
assistance programs to develop essential skills in note-taking, study systems,
time management, exam preparation, and research skills and to increase
reading rate and comprehension. In addition to these traditional kinds of
learning support services, the unique needs of each of these groups will have

A. S. Algier, K. W. Algier (Eds.). *New Directions for College Learning Assistance:
Reading and Study Skills*, no. 8. San Francisco: Jossey-Bass, June 1982

to be identified if adequate success opportunities are to be offered to these students. Reading-study skill centers, developmental studies, and the other organizational structures now responsible for aiding students in these traditional areas appear to be a likely resource that can be further developed to meet these special needs. Because of their rich, unique backgrounds, the professionals involved in these organizational components will constitute an excellent pool of leaders for this effort. The staffs of existing learning centers should become aware of the new market sectors most likely to be served by their institutions and prepare for those groups.

In almost all community colleges, regional and state universities, and many urban institutions, adult learners—the over twenty-five age group—will be numerous. Any students who have been away from the classroom for a number of years could very easily have the same needs. Learning center personnel should not only play a role in skill building and anxiety reduction for these students, but they also can serve as a resource for faculty in meeting the needs of these special students.

Adult students, who usually are more mature in attitude, seem to respond well to individualized, self-paced instruction as well as to short, concentrated courses. These are instructional styles in which staffs of learning centers have experience. As a result, they could provide valuable assistance to faculty within the various disciplines and subject areas in order to serve this clientele effectively.

The reasons for attending postsecondary institutions among the members of this group are particularly varied, as well as different from those of traditional students. The practitioner must start with a recognition of the adult learner's various motivations and a willingness to deal with them.

Motivating Factors

Returning adult students are a highly diverse group. The subgroups within this population exhibit distinctive needs, which reflect their present life situations. The motives and needs that impel them to seek further education are interwoven with the many aspects of their present living and past experiences (Boshier and Peters, 1976). Their socioeconomic status and their social and family roles greatly influence their reasons for becoming students. These reasons affect the problems and needs that they have and the services that they desire. Persons returning to school after years of absence fall into three broad categories: funded students (federal and state grants, CETA, public aid, and so forth), newly single adults, and married adults. Each category presents particular problems for the institution desiring to serve its members. In addition, all three groups also present problems common to older students. In designing programs and services to meet the needs of these students, attention must be paid both to their unique and to their common problems and needs.

Funded Adults. Funded adult students usually attend school because some agency has agreed to pay their expenses. There are always requirements, regulations, and expectations in exchange for this subsidy, and these stipulations often add to the problems already inherent in adult life situations. Requirements, such as full-time study and restrictions to courses that lead to a degree or to occupational courses, coupled with limits on the semesters of funding, create additional problems for adults with inadequate academic skills, poor self-concept, family responsibilities, and financial crises. Many of thse students become workaholics. Others seem satisfied to accomplish only what they must in order to continue receiving their checks.

Newly Single Adults. Newly single adult women often arrive at an educational institution with feelings of desperation and fear. Many aspects of their lives are in turmoil. Many times, they are faced with the prospect of having to support themselves and, frequently, children as well. This prospect forces them to make career decisions. They seek to learn skills that will enable them to become employed as quickly as possible. The emotional strain and changes in their life situation make study and learning extremely difficult. In contrast, many newly single men who attend postsecondary institutions seem to be seeking only social stimulation.

Married Adults. One finds the most diverse reasons for returning to school among married adults. Young married women are often seeking to begin or to complete career preparations that will satisfy personal or economic needs. Middle-aged and older women are often bored or seeking answers to questions of identity and self-fulfillment. Middle-aged men are trying to improve present career opportunities or begin new careers. Men and women of retirement age are seeking to build job skills that can help them to supplement inadequate pensions or achieve life goals.

Older students almost always come to the educational institution in a crisis. It may be an economic, identity, midlife, or transition crisis, but because of it their needs are acute. These needs, combined with these motives and academic, social, and cultural backgrounds, make challenging demands both on the institution and on learning assistance professionals.

Influences of Past Experiences

Academic Experiences. Within any one person's life, varied experiences greatly influence his or her perception of the academic environment and his or her ability to function in it. The adult's prior experiences with teachers, school administrators, and classmates as well as past classroom successes and failures affect the adult's level of confidence and comfort when approaching new learning experiences. Unpleasant or painful memories of past school experiences can make it difficult for adult learners to approach teachers or learning assistance personnel for information or help. Prior experiences in the academic environment influence adults in the cognitive domain as well. As with most other students, the extent and quality of prior education exerts considerable influence on an adult's ability to perform basic skills, such as reading, writing, and computation.

Prior social and cultural experiences are significant influences on the student's ability to achieve academically. The quality and quantity of these prior experiences are relevant to the student's prospects for academic success. Adults who have traveled widely; visited museums and historical places of interest; attended symphonies, lectures, and exhibits; read widely and diversely; and participated in civic and community organizations bring a very different store of information to the classroom than adults who have lived in rural isolation, who have not read a book since high school, and who have seldom traveled outside the county.

The attitudes of family and friends regarding education and their opinions about the adult's return to school exert a powerful influence on the adult student's academic achievement. Nonsupportive spouses and children are notorious saboteurs, particularly for women, whose primary family role has been to take care of everyone else, while putting themselves last. Overall, men have less difficulty in this respect, because improving one's career potential is viewed by society as admirable. The problems that are created when one family member begins to grow in confidence, independence, and sense of achievement have long been recognized in the mental health field. For some adult students, family conflict, combined with lack of peer support, can impair academic performance and even cause withdrawal from school.

Impact of the College Environment

Once an adult has made the decision to enroll in a formal learning program, several factors influence the likelihood of that adult's ever attending class and of staying in class. The initial encounter with college personnel greatly affects the extent to which the adult feels welcomed and accepted. Most adults will not tolerate being treated as adolescents. They will resist having to wait in long lines, wade through miles of red tape, and being snapped at by irritated or frustrated personnel. Older students expect to be treated with respect by other adults, whether they be admissions personnel, academic advisors, or custodians.

The availability or the absence of programs, services, and information designed for older learners is itself a statement of the institution's attitude toward adults as students. The presence of such support systems says, in more than words, "We want you here" and "You are important to us." Words of welcome that are not backed up by appropriate action are not believed for long.

The attitudes and behaviors of faculty members toward adult students are crucial both for student success and for their continuing as students (Apps, 1981). Older students are less tolerant than traditional students of poor teaching, unconcerned instructors, authoritarian and dictatorial teachers, and uncompromising requirements. Some teachers "find it difficult to descend from their lofty pedestal and treat their students as peers" (Apps, 1981, p. 73). Robbins, Mangano, and Corrado (1980) found that adult students expessed a preference for relaxed and informal instructors who provided alternate assignments and retests, incorporated audiovisual materials into instruction, and used student input to design and organize courses. They also expressed a high need for flexible attendance requirements. Effective teaching of adult students requires an awareness of and attention to the characteristics of adult students that set them apart from students of traditional age.

Adults as Students

Adults are students by choice. It takes considerable courage and an investment both of their time and their money (usually at the expense of their family) to become students. They have specific reasons for returning to school. Education is serious business, and they are willing to work hard to achieve their goals and justify their investment. Instructors report that adult students in their classes are highly motivated and goal-oriented. They want to perform well and to succeed as students. They set very high—sometimes unrealistically high—expectations both for themselves and for their instructors. An adult student who has arranged child care and driven thirty miles to campus only to find a class cancelled note on the lecture room door or a closed learning resources center is much more critical and vocal than the traditional student, who often responds with joy.

Older students who have been away from the classroom for a number of years experience varying degrees of fear, apprehension, and self-doubt. They are often unduly pessimistic about their own academic competencies and abilities. They fear competition with younger students, whom they view as more intelligent, assertive, and competent in the cognitive domain. They often feel self-conscious and embarrassed about their perceived inadequacies, and they tend to avoid subjects in which they anticipate failure.

Often, adult students are confused by the information on courses, credits, prerequisites, majors, and minors and by the terminology of college brochures and catalogues. Moreover, they are frequently unaware of learning assistance services, because they do not understand that they are eligible for such services. More often than not, they are embarrassed to ask for clarification or interpretation.

Adults have outside responsibilities imposed by families and jobs that make expected and unexpected demands on their time and energy.

Their role as a student is usually not their primary role. Management of time to meet both student and outside responsibilities is reported by most adult students to be their most difficult task.

Assistance in Improving Academic Performance

As a result of their intense desire to succeed and their need to accomplish much in limited time, adult students greatly need assistance in learning how to read faster and more comprehensively, how to study effectively and efficiently, how to write papers, how to take notes, how to take exams, how to reduce test anxiety, how to memorize, how to concentrate, and how to analyze and critique. In addition to these skills, a working knowledge of math and science is a prerequisite for many required and desired courses.

Many adults entering college feel very anxious about their ability to perform adequately. Much of their lack of self-confidence stems from their perceived incompetence and inability in cognitive areas. Cross (1981, p. 133) suggests that "one of the things that educators can do to encourage those with low levels of self-confidence about their ability to participate successfully in adult learning is to create more educational opportunities with low levels of risk and threat." She stresses that remedial programs should be noncompetitive and nonthreatening. Learning tasks should be clearly defined, and there should be adequate feedback and instruction for improvement. The objective of such opportunities is to demonstrate to anxious and fearful older students that they can succeed. Reading-study skills centers, noncredit and developmental courses, and remedial courses and workshops are safe and effective ways in which new adult students can assess the level of their present skills and improve their academic abilities.

In addition, tutors and peer assistants of similar age can often be helpful to adult students who experience academic difficulties. Further, support groups, professional counselors, and peer counselors can help adult students to resolve the crises that bring them to the institution. Many older students will request a place where they can study with their peers over a cup of coffee without having to endure loud, popular music.

Learning assistance personnel are the key to providing the programs and services that adult students need in order to achieve academically. Moreover, such programs and services serve to attract other adults, whose fears and anxieties have prevented them from approaching the institution. Programs that accommodate the needs of adult students stand to grow not only in the numbers that they serve but in the gratitude that they receive for their services.

References

Apps, J. W. *The Adult Learner on Campus: A Guide for Instructors and Administrators.* Chicago: Follett, 1981.

Boshier, R., and Peters, J. M. "Adult Needs, Interests, and Motives." In C. Klevins (Ed.), *Materials and Methods in Continuing Education.* Los Angeles: Klevins, 1976.

Carnegie Council on Policy Studies in Higher Education. *Three Thousand Futures: The Next Twenty Years for Higher Education.* San Francisco: Jossey-Bass, 1980.

Cross, K. P. *Adults as Learners: Increasing Participation and Facilitating Learning.* San Francisco: Jossey-Bass, 1981.

Robbins, W. A., Mangano, J. A., and Corrado, T. J. "Strategies for Serving the Reentry Adult Student in Community Colleges." *Catalyst,* 1980, *10* (3), 21–25.

Suzanne Teegarden is director of nontraditional and evening programs at John A. Logan College, Carterville, Illinois, where, until recently, she was coordinator of adult re-entry programs. Presently, she is pursuing doctoral studies in educational leadership at Southern Illinois University, Carbondale.

Robert E. Tarvin is president of John A. Logan College, a position he accepted at age twenty-eight in 1974, which made him one of the youngest college presidents in the nation. He has held numerous leadership positions in regional and state organizations, and in 1981, he was selected by Phi Delta Kappa as one of seventy-five outstanding young leaders in education.

One of the challenges to educators in the eighties will be to redefine the study skills needed to meet curricular demands.

Study Skills and Students of the Eighties

Ernest W. Tompkins

Economists, sociologists, and futurists will have their work cut out for them, but the real challenge in the 1980s will be to educators. The eighties will see a continuing explosion of information, ideas, and technical media for sharing ideas the thoughts. Dale Parnell (1981), President of the American Association of Community and Junior Colleges, stated that a major restructuring is going on in our country: "We are moving from mass communication and mass production to more individualized and specific approaches . . . and more decentralization." (Parnell, 1981, p. 2).

The educational community is facing budget cuts that limit resources and frustrate energy. In this situation, three questions should be considered by educators: Who are the students of the eighties? What study skills do these students need? What are the issues related to study skills and students of the eighties?

Who Are the Students of the Eighties?

Much of the literature and research on future students indicates that many students of the eighties will be employed older adults. According to Henderson and Plummer (1978), the number of high school graduates will decrease between 14 and 15 percent by 1985. They point out that high

A. S. Algier, K. W. Algier (Eds.). *New Directions for College Learning Assistance: Reading and Study Skills,* no. 8. San Francisco: Jossey-Bass, June 1982

school graduates are delaying college entry for several years. Zarakov (in Cacciola, 1979) believes that, unless community colleges adapt to the increasing numbers of nontraditional students, they could lose an estimated eleven million students over age thirty-five expected to be studying in the early 1980s.

A study of North Carolina community colleges by North Carolina State University (Shearon and others, 1980) indicates that most students in this fifty-eight institution system are employed adults with family responsibilities. The median ages are twenty-five and thirty-eight, respectively, for curriculum and continuing education students. More of these students are female—54 percent of the curriculum students and 71 percent of the continuing education students—and only about half of these students attend classes during the day.

The U.S. Bureau of the Census estimates fix the number of adults at twenty-two and older by 1985 at 155 million (Cross, 1981a). The National Center for Educational Statistics has projected that between 11.2 and 14.6 million students will be enrolled in college by 1985 (Henderson and Plummer, 1978). Cross (1981a) estimates that one third or more of all the current population participates in some form of organized instruction each year. Eaton (1981, p. 9) states that the students of tomorrow's colleges will be "seasoned, sophisticated, practical, and for the most part, undereducated."

Roueche (1981–1982, p. 17) states that not only will future students be older, more experienced, and more diverse by race and ethnicity, but "they will further be characterized by their collective inabilities to read, write, speak, listen, figure, and study well enough to pursue regular college level courses." As a result, they will need one semester or more of developmental education.

The implication of these views and projections is that nontraditional students will bring experiences from their previous roles to the learning activity. Job demands will restrict their time, and they will need flexibility in scheduling. They will need to develop study skills. Educators will need to attend both to the location of classes and to alternate delivery systems. Eaton (1981) predicts that services will be community-based, with the institution perceived as an education lending library in which students "check out" a course or two, stay away for a year or so, and return. Attention must be given to the information and counseling services available to these adult learners.

What Study Skills Are Needed for the Eighties?

In an address to the New York College Learning Skills Association Conference in November 1981, Patricia Cross said that there will be a close look in the 1980s at the purposes of admissions, with a focus on excellence, and that decisions will then have to be made concerning the practices needed to obtain excellence (Cross, 1981b). She cited Miami Dade's effort to merge quantity of enrollments with quality of learning for each student. The efforts at Miami Dade Community College place the responsibility for learning on the student, since what is expected of students is explained to them carefully. Cross emphasized the need for a conceptual change in institutions of higher learning whereby students are given an opportunity to work for an education, not a guarantee of a degree; where students are both supported in their work and expected to do their work; and where there is equal access and equal quality education.

One of the challenges to educators in the eighties will be to redefine the study skills needed to meet curricular demands. If by *study skills* we literally mean skills that enable students to study and thereby to learn, then the traditional definition of study skills must be expanded. What are some skills now needed to obtain excellence?

Basic Communication Skills. Communication skills (listening, viewing, speaking, and reading) affect the quality of life. About 70 percent of a person's day is spent communicating (Gayle, 1982). With the technology boom, the options for listening and viewing are limitless. The need for reading skills will not diminish. In fact, as the technical jargon in textbooks increases, there is already a greater demand for high verbal skills. According to Roueche (1981–1982), verbal requirements, especially in trade and technical courses, have almost doubled over the past fifteen to twenty years. Further, "in several recent college studies to determine readability levels of texts and trade manuals, only one course in 50 has written materials below 12th grade reading levels" (Roueche, 1981–1982, p.   ). Studies done at the University of Texas determined that today's high school graduate with a B average reads below the eighth-grade level, while many of the nation's Phi Beta Kappa baccalaureate graduates cannot read or write well enough to begin graduate or professional school (Roueche, 1981–1982).

To deal with the problem of ill-prepared precollege students, the California State Postsecondary Education Commissions (1980) suggested two options: adding a precollege year for remediation, or encouraging overprepared high school students to leave high school after the tenth or eleventh grade to go to college. In the latter case, the high school diploma could be awarded after successful completion of the first year of college.

Process-Orientated Skills. If the purpose of effective study skills is to learn or to obtain information, then problem-solving, computer literacy, and organizational skills will be important to the students of the eighties. With the rapid development of technology, computer literacy is a must. One developmental educator (Griffin, 1981) feels that skills in "systemic" thinking will be even more important than the three Rs. Systemic thinking is the capacity to see the whole as well as its parts—to see whole persons and their relationship to themselves and their world. Computer literacy will subsume systemic thinking.

With information available in a variety of formats—microcomputers, telecommunications, and microforms—more emphasis will need to be given to how to get information. It is apparent that the informational environment in the eighties will change continuously and dramatically (Haefner, 1982). One of the challenges to educators will be to explore the possibility that persons with a learning disability that prevents them from reading may be able to use such technology to learn—for example, by using a computer program or by watching a telecourse. The focus of such exploration would be on process: how to use microcomputers or telecommunications to receive information.

Computer literacy, which has been defined as whatever a person needs to know about computers and to be able to do with computers in order to function competently in society, is becoming a basic survival skill (Winkle and Matthews, 1982). One author (Melmed, 1982) feels that by 1990, every elementary and secondary student should spend an average of thirty minutes per day at a computer terminal and that these students should have access to at least 4,000 hours of computer courseware.

Preferred Learning Styles. The educator of the eighties should also be aware that different adult learners have different preferred learning styles. Studies indicate that adults prefer a variety of learning methods: "As many as 70 to 80 percent of respondents say they would prefer to learn by some method other than classroom lecture." Even tutors are more popular with older learners (Peterson, 1979, p. 124). Another study (Gayle, 1982) indicates that the retention rate by reading only is 10 percent; by listening only, 20 percent; by viewing only, 30 percent; by listening and viewing, 50 percent; by listening, viewing, and talking, 70 percent; and by listening, viewing, talking, and doing, 90 percent. A focus on process skills, the combination of creative instructional strategies, and the use of tutors and technology could create an exciting learning environment for students of the eighties. As Greene (1982, p. 329) states, "Our task is to move young people to be able to educate themselves and to create the kinds of classroom situations that stimulate them to do just that."

The challenge to meet the needs and demands of students of the eighties may seem overwhelming. But, just as policies and procedures have been developed in the past to deal with students' needs, so will tomorrow's educators also respond. Roueche (1981–1982) recommends four key policies related to meeting students' needs: First, time frame descriptions must be eliminated when describing community college programs of study. Second, working students must not be permitted to enroll for a full academic course load. Third, colleges and universities must begin serious assessment of students' skills when students arrive on the college campus. Fourth, not only must colleges assess students' learning skills, but they must also use data obtained from assessment to keep students out of college-level courses until students have demonstrated the abilities they need to succeed in such courses.

Issues Related to Study Skills and Students of the Eighties

Three issues related to study skills and students of the eighties are urgent: the influence of the information explosion, the influence of telecommunications and microcomputers, and the needs of special populations. It is not a question of whether new technology will be used but of how it can best be used to fulfill educational purposes. Educators will need to develop evaluation techniques that facilitate the effective use of available information and the effective choice of delivery systems.

The Information Explosion. Storing, retrieving, and processing information have been a central part of human activity since the beginning of time. According to Gayle (1982), a hundred books are published daily, and a hundred thousand technical journals are published yearly (this figure should double every fifteen years). For a child born in 1980, the knowledge available will increase four times by 1998; by 2030, this knowledge base will have increased thirty-two times.

The educator should try to understand the reality of the information explosion and its impact on education. With all this information available, the skill to evaluate what is the most pertinent and helpful will become essential to educators. Economics will play a part in the process if Gayle (1982) is correct: She predicts that picture books will cost an average of $25 by 1985, and that the average cost of a reference text will be $100 by 1990. In contrast, the average cost of a videodisc book or movie was only $15 in 1980. Haefner (1982) feels that the home computer will become a personal information and telecommunication system enabling its owner to retrieve and process information for personal needs.

Melmed ties the ideas of information explosion and technology development together with his discussion of information technology. By using information technology, "we can keep students actively engaged in learning for sustained periods, adjust teaching to the rate and learning style appropriate to the individual student, and provide a wide variety of direct problem-solving experiences through simulations and modeling" (Melmed, 1982, p. 309).

Telecommunications and Microcomputers. It is impossible to discuss the future without discussing technology. If the changes in technology and the information explosion make lifelong learning increasingly necessary, it seems safe to assume that they also will make it increasingly possible. Of particular importance to education is the increasing use of computerized toys, which already have a market share of some 20 percent (Haefner, 1982). Since the average household now has more than one television set, it is not difficult to see the impact that new developments in satellites, telecourses, and videodiscs will have on making the home into a learning center. Indeed, it will be possible for persons at home or in workplaces to obtain information from storage banks, libraries, and other agencies (Parnell, 1981). Gayle

(1982) asserts that people will be able to dial anything from the Library of Congress into their homes via videodisc by 1985. The thought that any document stored on microfilm in any library or reference collection in the world could be made available in one's home or workplace is astounding.

Telecommunications. One popular news weekly ("No Boob Tubes," 1981) suggested a motto for higher education in the eighties: "Give me your tired, your poor, your homebound masses yearning for a degree." The same source asserts that in fall 1981, 500 colleges were offering a total of nine courses for credit via 206 public television stations in conjunction with the Public Broadcasting Service. The courses were designed with students in mind who were full-time workers, housewives, handicapped adults, and people who lived as far as 400 miles from their chosen college. The courses can be taken individually or in groups that meet in homes, churches, public libraries, and college campuses.

Oshins (1981) has expressed some doubts about the use of television for instruction. He feels that the lack of direct faculty involvement, the lack of institutional involvement in course content and printed support materials, and the high front-end administrative costs militate against the use of television for instruction. He does feel, however, that television could be used effectively to teach specifics in thirty- or sixty-second spots, to attract interest for more involved study, and to inform people about higher education opportunities.

In contrast, Haefner (1982) feels that an interactive videotext system that combines the television set, the home computer, central computers, and centralized data storage via telephone lines will be widespread by the mid or late eighties. This system will make information readily available to everybody.

Microcomputers. Telephone surveys of all 15,442 U.S. school districts conducted between July and September 1981 indicate that 42 percent of these districts already use instructional computers and that 19 percent of the 84,226 public school buildings in the United States use computers for classroom instruction (Pritchard, 1982).

One of the biggest problems faced by schools that wish to use microcomputers is the lack of quality, field-tested courseware. Evaluations of large commercial courseware packages now on the market reveal that most of these packages are intended for supplementary drill and practice in the classroom; about 95 percent are arithmetic programs (Long, 1982). Empirical studies of drill-and-practice computer programs have found them to be consistently effective in arithmetic but less so in reading and language arts (Melmed, 1982).

Melmed (1982) lists three conditions that could delay full use of computers in the classroom: insufficient school budgets for instructional materials, inadequate inventory of available courseware, and inadequate funding for development of new approaches to student use of computers. Nevertheless, one former educator who founded a successful computer services firm (Long, 1982) feels that the software services industry will be the most exciting frontier for the U.S. in the 1980s.

Educators must remember that technologies have no power by themselves: They will be only what they are designed to be. Technology can intensify pressures already felt by educators. Haefner (1982) suggests that the integration of microcomputers in most of the more complex technology allows for many kinds of adaptive responses and that it gives people the feeling of being embedded in an "intelligent" environment. This feeling removes the burden of considering the interactions and reactions of a "stupid" system. Hunter and McCants (1977) point out that students now in their twenties have lived their entire lives in a world that does little to develop patience. Systems of information that are decades old are being displaced with the speed of light. Students' acceptance of immediate replays and pattern recognition leave little room for the patience and perseverance necessary to develop logic or even basic skills in reading and arithmetic: "Younger students are responding to the world in which they have been brought up by accepting its values—perfunctory recognition of authority figures, limited involvement, iconics, inanimates, and instant information retrieval—although not necessarily retaining for any length of time any of these" (Hunter and McCants, 1977, p. 3). Educators should be mindful of these influences on students of the eighties.

Parnell (1981) suggests that four major, positive shifts in education will result from new developments in technology: open access to learning; education for all, as opposed to education for each; emphasis on learning and what is to be learned, not on what is to be taught; and increased cooperative, consortial, and collaborative efforts.

The Needs of Special Populations. Most of the literature indicates that handicapped persons will receive much attention in the immediate future. Two factors could account for this focus: emphasis on the needs of handicapped Vietnam War veterans and compliance with Section 504 of the 1973 Vocational Rehabilitation Act, which mandates equal access for handicapped individuals.

The Community College of Denver has made a special effort to meet the needs of handicapped students (Bell, 1981). Of a total student population of 14,000, approximately 1,000 handicapped students now enroll each year. They attend regular classes and participate in campus activities. A center for the physically disadvantaged was established for these students. This center serves students with vocational evaluation, health services, instructional support, counseling, and job placement. Bell (1981, p. 38) feels that the key to his institution's success is "commitment over compliance."

In New Jersey, a telecollege has been established to assist persons confined to homes or institutions to take college courses (Coexeter, 1981). Telephones connect the off-campus student to regularly scheduled courses. Two-way classroom speakers enable students to participate in discussions.

It is obvious, of course, that physically handicapped students are most in need of equal physical access to learning institutions. Educators of the eighties need special training to deal with the complex problems that physically disabled students bring to the traditional classroom. Special training for educators should include strategies for alternative learning activities. Technology will aid in the instruction to deaf students, since microcomputers are capable of talking to them and for them.

For students with learning disabilities, telecommunications and microcomputers hold out promise. Documents identified by Cacciola (1979) may prove helpful to educators who want to learn about the materials and equipment needed to serve disabled students of two-year colleges.

Other special populations will include refugees from various foreign countries, persons institutionalized in hospitals and prisons, ex-felons, and the dependent children of college and university students. Sensitive and conscientious assessment of the needs of these populations will ease their entry or re-entry to education. The must urgent academic need of refugees is communication skills. Institutionalized persons may need coping skills. Ex-felons and students' dependents will need assistance in making the transition to the academic environment.

The conscientious educator will find the 1980s a challenge. The future can be created by looking forward to it, talking about it, and making plans to meet its demands.

References

Bell, A. R. "Access for the Disabled." *Community and Junior College Journal.* 1981, *52* (1), 37–38.

Cacciola, R. M. "Sources and Information: Special Programs for Special Populations." *New Directions for Community Colleges,* 1979, *3* (3), 91–100.

California State Postsecondary Education Commission. *Issues in Planning for the Eighties.* Sacramento: California State Postsecondary Education Commission, 1980.

Coexeter, B. "Telecollege for the Homebound." *Community and Junior College Journal.* 1981, *52* (1), 39–40.

Cross, K. P. *Adults as Learners: Increasing Participation and Facilitating Learning.* San Francisco: Jossey-Bass, 1981.

Cross, K. P. "On Old Practices and New Purposes in Education." An address to the New York College Learning Skills Association, Grossingers, N.Y., November 1981b.

Eaton, J. S. "Society 2000: Presidents and Prophecy." *Community and Junior College Journal.* 1981, *52* (1), 6–10.

Edwards, J. M. B. *American Higher Education to 1985.* Washington, D.C.: Educational Policy Research Center for Higher Education and Society. 1979. (ED 202 272).

Gayle, M. "2000 and Beyond: A Relevant Curriculum." A presentation to Phi Delta Kappa, Winston-Salem, N.C., January 1982.

Greene, M. "Literacy for What?" *Phi Delta Kappan.* 1982, *63* (5), 326–329.

Griffin, T. "One Point of View: The Expanding Future of Developmental Education." *Journal of Developmental and Remedial Education.* 1981, *5* (1), 26.

Haefner, K. "Challenge of Information Technology to Education: The New Educational Crisis." *T. H. E. Journal.* 1982, 47–49, 52.

Henderson, C., and Plummer, J. C. *Adapting to Changes in the Characteristics of College-Age Youth.* Policy Analysis Service Reports, Vol. 4, No. 2. Washington, D.C.: Policy Analysis Service, American Council on Education, 1978.

Hunter, W. E., and McCants, L. C. *The New Generation Gap: Involvement Versus Instant Information.* Topical Paper, No. 64. Los Angeles: ERIC Clearinghouse for Junior Colleges, 1977 (ED 148 412).

Long, S. M. "The Dawning of the Computer Age: An Interview With Ronald Palamara." *Phi Delta Kappan.* 1982, *63* (5), 311–313.

Melmed, A. S. "Information Technology for U.S. Schools." *Phi Delta Kappan.* 1982, *63* (5), 308–310.

"No Boob Tubes." *Time.* October 5, 1981, p. 46.

Oshins, J. H. "Snap, Crackle, and Pop: Learning from Television." *Change.* 1981, 8–10.

Parnell, D. "AACJC President's Column: Would the Apostle Paul Be Using the Satellite Today?" *Community and Junior College Journal.* 1981, *52* (3), 2–4.

Peterson, R. E., and associates. *Lifelong Learning in America.* San Francisco: Jossey-Bass Publishers, 1979.

Pritchard, W. H., Jr. "Instructional Computing in 2001: A Scenario." *Phi Delta Kappan.* 1982, *63* (5), 322–325.

Roueche, J. E. "Transfer and Attrition—Points of View: Don't Close the Door." *Community and Junior College Journal.* 1981–1982, *52* (4), 17, 21–23.

Shearon, R. W., and others. *Pulling Learning to Work: A Profile of Students in North Carolina Community Colleges, Technical Institutes, and Technical Colleges.* Raleigh: Department of Adult and Community College Education, North Carolina State University. 1980.

Winkle, L. W., and Matthews, W. M. "Computer Equity Comes of Age." *Phi Delta Kappan.* 1982, *63* (5), 314–315.

Ernest W. Tompkins is director of the Individualized Learning Center and administrator of the GED program at Forsyth Technical Institute in Winston-Salem, North Carolina.

The editors summarize the volume.

Concluding Comments

Ann S. Algier
Keith W. Algier

The reading required simply to survive the current information explosion intimidates and overwhelms college students. For this reason, they may have been more perceptive than university administrators in recognizing the need for study skills. That is the conclusion reached in a study by the National Institute of Education of entering freshmen (Roueche, 1978). Seventy percent acknowledged that they were deficient in study methods and that they felt a need to develop additional skills. This sourcebook has been designed to acquaint readers with the latest learning assistance theory and to suggest practical strategies for implementing successful academic support programs.

In the first chapter, Georgine Materniak contends that a new era of professionalism is emerging in the field of learning assistance with the interest in identifying theories that explain the underlying processes of the skills that good learning practitioners teach. She holds that the vitality of programs can be attributed to the combined efforts of specialists from diverse disciplines, but she argues that the field must develop a universal theoretical base if it is ever to evolve into a profession.

Analyses of successful reading-study skills programs by Vickie Sanders, Heath Lowry, and William Theime provide readers with guiding principles for program development. The authors identify content and operational factors that appear to be common in programs reporting

A. S. Algier, K. W. Algier (Eds.). *New Directions for College Learning Assistance: Reading and Study Skills,* no. 8. San Francisco: Jossey-Bass, June 1982

significant pre- and postest gains and improvement in grade point averages. The authors recommend additional research to measure variables that increase reading-study skills effectiveness.

The chapter by John Milton recognizes the responsibility that educators have in helping students to acquire skills that enable them to become independent learners. Milton suggests specific techniques for developing essential study skills.

Arthur Whimbey and John Glade point out that questions in tests of reading comprehension closely resemble questions in standard verbal intelligence tests. They offer examples of questions that call for analytical reasoning and demonstrate how practice in working with such items can result in improved reading comphrehension. They also discuss vocalized thinking as an approach to improving analytical reading and reasoning. By thinking aloud, students become more aware of inadequacies in reading and reasoning. The authors also offer opinions concerning speed-reading misconceptions.

According to Ann Algier, one justification for teaching students to survey textbooks is that individuals who can distill vast amounts of information for others will be in demand in the future. Study skills instructors should stress the importance of mastering survey procedures in textbook analysis. This author cites the value of learning how to use a survey system and suggests techniques for storing and retrieving information.

Listening comprehension is positively and significantly correlated with both grade point average and retention, according to Martha S. Conaway. She believes that listening comprehension can be taught, and toward that end she offers a number of practical suggestions for instructors. Conaway concludes that addition of listening courses to the curriculum would benefit both students and institutions concerned with student attrition.

David Hubin and Susan J. Lesyk illustrate the differences in examination preparation by passive and active learners. They emphasize that students must learn to question in order to analyze, synthesize, and organize course material for examinations. They use their research, which indicated that how information is stated in essay examinations appears to be as important as what is written, to describe some logical steps in prewriting.

Suzanne Teegarden and Robert E. Tarvin point out that special demands will be placed on institutions of higher learning in the closing years of the twentieth century to develop and support more learning assistance programs. They observe that the changing student population will require learning assistance programs that help them to develop essential skills in note-taking, study, time management, research, and exam preparation and to increase reading rate and comprehension. The authors are convinced that learning assistance personnel are key to the programs and services that adult students need. They contend that well-designed programs will attract students whose fears and anxieties have prevented them from entering institutions of higher learning.

Ernest Tompkins observes in his chapter that students of the eighties will be practical and sophisticated but probably undereducated and that andragogy, the art and science of helping adults learn, is properly becoming a concern of higher education. He believes that most students of the eighties will be employed, at least part-time. Consequently, they will be short of time and impatient. Teaching may become a matter of offering only what learners consider essential. The issue of computer literacy is also examined by this author.

All the authors seem to agree that reading is the one skill absolutely essential for success in college. The National Assessment of Educational Progress report comments that a society in which the habits of disciplined reading, analysis, interpretation, and discourse are not sufficiently cultivated has much to fear (*Reading, Thinking, and Writing*, 1981). However, teaching these skills should not be the sole responsibility of reading teachers. The greatest gains in reading are obtained when teachers of all disciplines reinforce study-reading strategies.

References

National Assessment of Educational Progress. *Reading, Thinking, and Writing: Results From the 1979–80 National Assessment of Reading and Literature.* Denver, Colo.: National Assessment of Educational Progress, 1981.
Roueche, John. Address to Jefferson Community College Faculty, June 1978.

Ann S. Algier is associate professor in the Department of Learning Skills, Eastern Kentucky University.

Keith W. Algier is professor of history at Eastern Kentucky University.

Index

DATE DUE

12·17·86			

DEMCO 38-297